Buddha Shakyamuni

GURU PADMASAMBHAVA

༉ །སེམས་དོན་དངོས་གཞིའི་ཉམས་ལེན་གནད་བསྡུས་
བཞུགས་སོ།

པདྨ་ཀུ་པའི་སྐུ་བསྐྱར་མཐུན་ཚོགས་ནས་
སྐུ་བསྐྱར་ཞུས།

The Padmakara Translation Group gratefully acknowledges the generous support of the Tsadra Foundation in sponsoring the translation and preparation of this book.

Practicing the Great Perfection

Instructions on the Crucial Points

Shechen Gyaltsap Gyurmé Pema Namgyal

TRANSLATED BY THE
Padmakara Translation Group

SHAMBHALA

Shambhala Publications, Inc.
4720 Walnut Street
Boulder, Colorado 80301
www.shambhala.com

© 2020 by the Padmakara Translation Group

Cover art: Guru Rinpoche giving an initiation in a cave. Detail from a set of late nineteenth-century thangkas depicting the eight aspects of Guru Padmasambhava. Photograph by Matthieu Ricard. Used with permission.

9 8 7 6 5 4 3 2 1

First edition

Printed in the United States of America

♾ This edition is printed on acid-free paper that meets the American National Standards Institute z39.48 Standard.
♻ Shambhala Publications makes every effort to print on recycled paper. For more information please visit www.shambhala.com.
Shambhala Publications is distributed worldwide by Penguin Random House, Inc., and its subsidiaries.

LIBRARY OF CONGRESS CATALOGING-IN-PUBLICATION DATA
Names: Gyaltsap, Shechen, author. | Comité de traduction Padmakara.
Title: Practicing the great perfection: instructions on the crucial points / Shechen Gyatsap Gyurmé Pema Namgyal; translated by the Padmakara Translation Group.
Description: Boulder, Colorado: Shambhala, 2020. |
Includes bibliographical references and index.
Identifiers: LCCN 2019045065 | ISBN 9781559394932
(trade paperback: acid-free paper)
Subjects: LCSH: Rdzogs-chen. | Rnying-ma-pa (Sect)—Texts. |
Perfection—Religious aspects—Buddhism.
Classification: LCC BQ7662.4 .G923 2020 | DDC 294.3/444—dc23
LC record available at https://lccn.loc.gov/2019045065

Contents

FOREWORD

Reading these mind teachings of the most precious and kind master Shechen Gyaltsap Gyurmé Pema Namgyal brings back such powerful memories of the way Kyabje Dilgo Khyentse Rinpoche, my beloved grandfather and root teacher, used to explain the illusory nature of the self, undermining our ego-clinging, as a means to introducing us to the nature of the mind. Of course, the striking similarity of approach is not surprising when one remembers the unfathomable devotion that Khyentse Rinpoche had throughout his life for Gyaltsap Rinpoche, his root teacher.

When Khyentse Rinpoche was little more than thirteen years old, Gyaltsap Rinpoche introduced him to the nature of his mind, using verses taken from the *Prayer to Guru Rinpoche in Seven Chapters*, in particular the words,

> Outwardly, the things that are perceived are pure.
> Inwardly, the mind itself perceiving them is free and open.
> Between these two, just recognize the state of luminosity.
> Through compassion of the Buddhas, past, present, and to
>   come,
> May our minds be blessed and freed.

Saying this, and with his hand in the mudra of subduing phenomenal appearances, Gyaltsap Rinpoche looked directly at Khyentse Rinpoche and with a solemn and impressive voice asked three times, "What is your mind?" And at that moment, Khyentse Rinpoche had the unshakable conviction that his teacher was Guru Rinpoche in person. Rinpoche once told me that, out of respect for his root master, he would never dare to use these same verses to introduce his own students to the nature of the mind.

I am extremely grateful that Helena and Wulstan, both close disciples of Dilgo Khyentse Rinpoche, have given us this beautiful, limpid, and inspiring translation of these precious teachings. We have been given a priceless treasure. It is now up to us to put it into practice.

The Seventh Shechen Rabjam
Shechen Monastery, Nepal, May 2019

TRANSLATORS' INTRODUCTION

Shechen Gyaltsap Gyurmé Pema Namgyal, the author of this short collection of essential instructions, was born in the iron sheep year of the fifteenth sexagenary cycle (*rabjung*) (1871) in the region of Dergé, in Eastern Tibet. He received his birth name from his father, Adro Sherab, a hidden yogi of high accomplishment.[1] Shortly after his birth, the young child was unanimously recognized by numerous important lamas of the Nyingma school as the rebirth of Orgyen Rangjung, the second Shechen Gyaltsap.[2] "Even if he were to be examined a hundred times," Jamyang Khyentse Wangpo declared, "no error would be found." He was duly enthroned and received the name Gyurmé Pema Tendzin Khedrup Gyatso'i Dé. Later, on receiving his first monastic vows from Dzogchen Khenpo Damchö Özer, he was given the name Gyurmé Pema Namgyal, by which he is more generally known.

As one might expect, Shechen Gyaltsap's birth and early youth were attended by numerous auspicious signs. In particular, it is recorded that the bodhisattva instinct and the habits of compassion were so strong in him that from his earliest years, far from ever consuming meat, he could not bear even its taste or smell. Dilgo Khyentse Rinpoche records that simply to drink soup made in vessels that had been used to cook meat would, it seems, produce an allergic reaction in his mouth. This may well have been regarded as one of the authenticating signs of his identity since it was recorded that the previous incarnation had often remarked on the faults of eating the flesh of animals slaughtered for food, the consumption of which he considered to be the cause of the illnesses that were to shorten his life. In any case, like the famous Shabkar Tsogdruk Rangdrol and Patrul Rinpoche before him, Shechen

Gyaltsap abstained from meat throughout his life, and this was no mean accomplishment in the cold highlands of Kham, where the only alternative foods were dairy products, tsampa flour made from roasted barley grains, and the sparse vegetables imported from lower, more fertile regions.

Shechen Gyaltsap received full ordination from Gemang Khenpo Yönten Gyatso, otherwise known as Khenpo Yönga, the author of the celebrated three-volume commentary on Jigme Lingpa's *Treasury of Precious Qualities*. Natural inclination disposed him to monastic discipline, and he maintained a lifelong and utterly unblemished observance of the vows. Having gone forth into homelessness, to use the traditional expression, it is said that he never again crossed the threshold of a layperson's house. His life henceforth consisted of study, teaching, and prolonged meditative practice.

Endowed with a keen intelligence, a prodigious memory, and a natural inclination to study, he immersed himself in the world of Tibetan scholarship and practice, which in his day had been brought to vigorous life by the *rimé*, or nonsectarian, movement then in full flower in the eastern regions of Tibet. This great religious, intellectual, and social initiative had been set in motion in the generation preceding Shechen Gyaltsap's birth by Jamyang Khyentse Wangpo, Jamgön Kongtrul Lodrö Thayé, Chogyur Dechen Lingpa, Patrul Rinpoche, and their disciples: Mipham Rinpoche, Gemang Khenpo Yönten Gyatso, Minyak Kunzang Sonam, and others. Its aim was to revive and restore the Buddhist teachings generally, and in particular, to preserve and foster the traditions of the older schools—Nyingma, Sakya, and Kagyu—many of which were in an advanced state of decline. In so doing, its declared purpose was to recover an attitude of open, respectful, eclectic inquiry between the different schools of Tibetan Buddhism of the kind that had characterized an earlier age before the intellectual and religious climate had been overshadowed and soured by almost two centuries of oppressive, sectarian intolerance.

Important centers of learning were restored or founded anew, and great collections of texts were assembled, edited, and published.

Together with many of his contemporaries—Khenpo Kunzang Pelden, Kathok Situ, the fifth Shechen Rabjam, and others—Shechen Gyaltsap participated fully in this important and influential movement. Jamyang Khyentse Wangpo, Jamgön Kongtrul, and Mipham Rinpoche were among his principal teachers. His studies were wide ranging and included texts of all schools of Tibetan Buddhism: the *Treasury of Logic*[3] by Sakya Pandita, the *Great Exposition of the Stages of the Path*[4] by Je Tsongkhapa, the writings of Karma Rangjung Dorje, and so on. Nevertheless, Shechen Gyaltsap's main affiliation was with the Nyingma school, and his biographies contain long lists of the texts he studied and the transmissions he received. He was, in particular, one of the closest disciples of Mipham Rinpoche and became himself a scholar of vast erudition. It was moreover with reference to his love of learning that, shortly before Mipham's death, Mipham bequeathed to him all his books and writings. Together with Kunzang Pelden and Kathok Situ, Shechen Gyaltsap was responsible for the assembly of Mipham's collected works and the establishment of their reading transmission (*lung*). He therefore played a crucial role in the preservation of the unique teaching tradition of Mipham Rinpoche, a magisterial synthesis and restatement of the sutra and tantra teachings of the Nyingma school reaching back through the writings of Jigme Lingpa, Longchen Rabjam, and Rongzom Pandita, to Śāntarakṣita and Guru Rinpoche, the original founding fathers of Tibetan Buddhism.

After the destruction of the Tibetan monasteries in the wake of the Chinese communist invasion and the ensuing Cultural Revolution, Shechen Gyaltsap's collected writings were reassembled in Bhutan in the late 1970s under the auspices of one of his most famous disciples, Dilgo Khyentse Rinpoche. This collection came to nineteen Tibetan volumes and has recently been reedited and published in Taiwan in thirteen large Western-style books. This collection, which contains works covering the entire range of sutra and tantra, remains largely unknown to Western readers. Chatral Rinpoche, who held Shechen Gyaltsap in the highest regard, would refer to his collected works as a "wish-fulfilling treasure," and declared that among all the Nyingma writers of the present age, his works were of the greatest clarity and importance. The first of Shechen Gyaltsap's works to be brought out of Tibet was *The Chariot of Liberation*, his great commentary on the tantric preliminary practice. When Dilgo Khyentse Rinpoche received it, he placed it on his head and declared that it was worth more than all the gold in the entire world.[5]

Like Mipham Rinpoche, Shechen Gyaltsap spent most of his life in solitude, engaged either in study, composition, or meditative retreat—emerging only to give transmissions and empowerments, to teach his close disciples, or receive important guests.

His principal hermitage, ruined during the Cultural Revolution but now restored, may still be visited high on the mountain-side above the Shechen retreat center, itself a steep climb above the monastery. From the window of what was once his room—a small space accommodating a simple bed, seat, and shrine—one can look down to the valley floor far below and the temples and monastic buildings now richly restored, or else across the high, desolate hills of Kham to the south and west.

Several stories attest to the greatness of Shechen Gyaltsap's spiritual attainment. It is recorded that he was once instructed by Jamyang Khyentse Wangpo to make a long retreat on Vajrakilaya and to practice until all the signs of accomplishment had manifested. After only one hundred days, Shechen Gyaltsap concluded his retreat and performed the traditional fire ceremony, saying that the practice was complete. He noticed that, as one of the signs of attainment, he had left the print of his foot on a rock by the door of his hermitage. Not wanting others to see it, he threw the stone far away, though it was later recovered by one of his disciples.[6] And after his death, during the cremation ceremony, eyewitnesses reported that his body completely vanished in the flames and left

Shechen hermitages. The topmost hermitage is the one
where Shechen Gyaltsap lived. Photo courtesy of
Matthieu Ricard.

no trace but that wherever the smoke of the fire settled on the trees and bushes in the surrounding area, crystalline relics (*rinsel*) were found.

Although photography was known in Tibet during Shechen Gyaltsap's lifetime and photographs were taken of many of his contemporaries—Kathok Situ and the sixth Shechen Rabjam, for example—Shechen Gyaltsap always refused to have his picture taken, no doubt influenced by Mipham Rinpoche, who regarded the modern camera with great suspicion.[7] The misfortune of thus having no record of Shechen Gyaltsap's physical appearance is nevertheless compensated to some extent by the personal reminiscences of Dilgo Khyentse Rinpoche recorded in his own autobiography.[8] The two lamas first met in 1912 when Shechen Gyaltsap visited Denkhok for the funeral ceremonies for Mipham Rinpoche. At that time, Khyentse Rinpoche was two years old, and it was only in 1924, at the age of fourteen, that he actually went to Shechen and received teachings. Gyaltsap Rinpoche died in 1926, and so it was that the meeting between master and disciple lasted for only two years. That short but intense encounter left an indelible mark on Khyentse Rinpoche's life. It was Shechen Gyaltsap who enthroned him as the incarnation of Jamyang Khyentse Wangpo, gave him the *śramanera* ordination according to the lower Vinaya lineage,[9] and bestowed on him innumerable empowerments and teaching transmissions.

Like many accomplished masters of the Great Perfection, Shechen Gyaltsap was a man of great personal warmth and simplicity. Khyentse Rinpoche recalled his kindness and how he took delight in the presence of children. He was always considerate and soft-spoken, and during empowerments and on other occasions, he would play and joke with the young tulkus and monks and tell them stories.[10] Everyone must have loved him. It was from Shechen Gyaltsap that Khyentse Rinpoche first imbibed the habits of study and learning, and it was from him that he received early encouragement in the cultivation of his poetic skills. Nevertheless, there seems little doubt that it was as a master of the Great Perfection that Shechen Gyaltsap exerted the greatest influence on his young disciple. Indeed, he introduced him to the nature of the mind, with the result that despite the shortness of their time together, Khyentse Rinpoche considered him his most revered root teacher.

> Generally speaking, my teacher Shechen Gyaltsap appeared to genuinely possess all the qualifications of a master that are taught in the sutras and tantras, and he was especially grounded in the experience of the highest view of the Great Perfection as it is. Subsequently, when I studied, reflected, and pretended to teach these aspects, I felt that having the good fortune to actually receive such a golden doctrine like a wish-fulfilling gem from my precious master, the perfect Buddha, made gaining a human birth worthwhile, and I felt even more devoted and inspired than usual. Even nowadays, while pretending to teach these aspects, I keep my precious master in mind . . . and invoke him to make the exposition and study meaningful.[11]

In later years, when speaking of his beloved master, Khyentse Rinpoche, as a mark of respect, would never presume even to mention his name but would always refer to him as *Kadrinchen*, "the one who was most kind."[12]

With the exception of the fourth and fifth instructions of the present collection, which are mainly theoretical expositions, the texts collected here are essential instructions designed for those who practice, or aspire to practice, the teachings of the Great Perfection. They are not intended for the general reader but for those who have received initiation and instruction from a qualified master of the lineage. In many ways, they are very simple or, to be more exact, are expressed with a simplicity that belies their great profundity. They are brief and to the point, often referring to more extensive teachings of which the experienced practitioner is naturally expected to be aware. Mainly belonging to the level of the "cutting through" (*trekchö, khregs chod*) teachings of the Great Perfection, they give direct and practical advice on how the yogi or yogini should meditate and behave in ordinary life. They begin with an extensive reflection on the problem of self-clinging and the analytical meditation designed to uproot it, and proceed to more specific instructions for the mind practice itself, at all times insisting on the fundamental, indispensable attitudes of renunciation and bodhichitta.

In two of the instructions, Shechen Gyaltsap quotes extensively from the writings of Sherab Yarphel, and indeed there are two instructions devoted entirely to the teachings of this great master. In his biography of Shechen Gyaltsap, Dilgo Khyentse Rinpoche records that Sherab Yarphel was the immediate predecessor, in the line of incarnation, of Jamgön Kongtrul. He was a disciple of Pema Sangak Tendzin Chögyal, the first Shechen Gyaltsap,[13] and became one of the thirteen great siddhas or *drupthop* (*grub thob*)[14] of Shechen. By the age of nineteen, he had accumulated one hundred million recitations of the *mani* mantra. A monk of strict observance, he never touched gold or precious substances, and apart from a pilgrimage to central Tibet at the age of twenty, he spent his entire life in Dechen Pema Öling, the retreat center of Shechen, living in the retreat place that Shechen Gyaltsap was later to use as his own hermitage. Until the age of thirty, he engaged in generation-stage practice, completing vast accumulations of mantra recitation, as well as in the yogas of the perfection stage. He is said to have experienced bliss, luminosity, and no-thought over a period of nine years and, thanks to the strength of his devotion for his teacher, to have realized the nature of his mind at the age of thirty. From that moment onward, he focused exclusively on guru yoga and the practice of primordial purity and spontaneous presence belonging to the teachings of the Great Perfection. He actualized the primordial wisdom of the four visions of *thögal* and reached at last the everlasting state of the dharmakāya. Many external signs attested to his perfect attainment. He left numerous handprints and footprints in the rocks, his clairvoyance was unimpaired, and he was able to see directly into the minds of others. After his death, many claimed that his relics had the power to protect them from all external dangers. His wealth of realization overflowed into literary composition, and he is said to have left four or five volumes of writings. These unfortunately were never properly assembled and published, and were eventually lost. It is said that even in the time when Khyentse Rinpoche was still in Tibet, only one short collection of songs of realization and practice instructions had survived; and perhaps by now these too have vanished into oblivion. The texts quoted by Shechen Gyaltsap in the present book may therefore be the only surviving compositions of that great Dzogchen yogi.

ACKNOWLEDGMENTS

This translation could not have been made without the inspiration of our lamas, Pema Wangyal Rinpoche and Jigme Khyentse Rinpoche, and without the advice and help of Khenchen Pema Sherab of Namdroling monastery, Mysore, India. We would like to express our special thanks to them and to Gelong Konchok Tendzin (Matthieu Ricard), for his helpful information concerning Shechen monastery and the persons mentioned by Gyaltsap Rinpoche, as well as for his reminiscences of Dilgo Khyentse Rinpoche and his permission to use his photograph of Gyaltsap Rinpoche's hermitage. This text was translated by Helena Blankleder and Wulstan Fletcher of the Padmakara Translation Group.

PRACTICING THE GREAT PERFECTION

The Brilliant Lamp

A Summary of the Crucial Points of Mind Practice

Namo Guru Mañjuśrīye!

To the Dharmakāya Vajradhara,
To my teacher never parted from him,
I prostrate in reverence with my body, speech, and mind.
A clear, essential distillation
Of the crucial points of practice I shall now compose.

Prepare yourself by receiving empowerment, keeping *samaya*, and purifying your mind stream according to the common and uncommon paths of the Mahāyāna.[15] I, for my part, will give a very easy explanation of how the two kinds of no-self are established.

When you shoot an arrow, you first need to see your target. In the same way, you need to identify the root of imputation: that to which the innate sense of self, or "I," the conceived object[16] of self-clinging, is ascribed. This "I," or self, is not found to exist in the sense objects of the outer world; no one calls them "I." Similarly, no one considers the collection of five aggregates, the body and mind, of other people as "I." For they are regarded as other. To what therefore is the notion "I" imputed?

There are various standpoints from which to consider one's self-identity, or "I." It might be in terms of sexual status—whether one is male or female or neither—or it might be in terms of one's family lineage and so on. Be that as it may, the root of the imputation of self is generally thought to reside in three items gathered within one's own continuum: one's body, one's mind, and one's name. The self must be found somewhere within them. It is impossible for it to be anywhere else.

Now how is "I" apprehended in these three items? The feeling "I am ill," for instance, occurs in relation to the body—that is, to any of its five solid, or six hollow, organs.[17] The same applies to the external surface of the body, beginning with the tips of the hairs on one's head to the nails on one's toes—all the members and secondary members of the body. One only has to be touched by a spark of fire or pierced by a thorn and one feels, "It wounded *me*; it burned *me*; *I* have been hurt." Likewise in the mind—whether prompted by external circumstances or not—one clings to a sense of self, thinking "Today *I'm* happy; today *I'm* sad; *I* understand what's going on; *I* don't understand." Something similar occurs with regard to one's name—whether it was given by one's parents or one's abbot or teacher. Whenever someone calls this name, one thinks, "They are calling *me*; they are talking to *me*; they are saying something nice to *me*; they are insulting *me*."

So it is that "I" is identified equally with these three items (body, mind, and name). And on the basis of this ego-clinging, the defilements of craving and so on occur. These, in turn, give rise to action, from which the entire mass of samsaric suffering results. So it is that the root of existence, or samsara, comes down to one's innate clinging to "I."

Now, ordinary beings, whose minds are unaffected by the study of tenets, do not [as a matter of fact] apprehend a permanent, single, autonomous self of the kind talked about in non-Buddhist systems. A self of this kind is disproved by direct perception. For the experiences of happiness, sadness, and so on are apprehended occasionally—which shows that the self [the subject of these experiences] is not permanent.[18] Since it is apprehended in different ways, it cannot be regarded as single or discrete. And since the "I," or self, depends on [and is affected by] situations of pleasure, pain, and so on, it is not independent or autonomous. Neither is it the case that one has a self that has existed from before and that will cease to exist sometime in the future. For if one searches for what one calls one's self, nothing is found.

If this "I," or self—the conceived object of innate self-clinging and the root of samsaric existence—does exist, it must be found somewhere in the three items just mentioned: body, mind, and name. Let us therefore examine them.

The body is by nature an assemblage of several items grouped together—that is, its main and secondary members. But if it is gradually dissected [into smaller and smaller parts], one reaches a point beyond which one cannot go: the infinitesimal, partless particles, which are the ultimate range, or limit, of the form aggregate. The mind, on the other hand, consists of the eight consciousnesses and the mental factors. Moreover, each of the four mental aggregates of feeling, perception, conditioning factors, and consciousness also consists of a multiplicity according to its particular objects and associated mental aspects. But once again, the mind itself cannot be broken down and analyzed beyond the indivisible moments of consciousness that constitute it. As for names, these are nonassociated conditioning factors (*ldan min 'du byed*),[19] which are imputed or labeled adventitiously only when inanimate objects and conscious minds are brought together. On the other hand, if a search is made for the object labeled, nothing will be found—it has no existence whatsoever. And this is the case with all names, patronymics, and so on.

By examining and thinking in this way, one can see that the infinitesimal particles of matter and the instants of consciousness do not constitute the self, because they do not correspond to the self in the way that it has been defined [as permanent, single, and autonomous]. For example, they are impermanent: they cease and transform at every instant. The single partless particles and the individual instants of consciousness cannot be taken for the self either. For if they were, there would be an infinite number of selves. It might be thought that the self consists of the gathering together and combination of all these material particles and instants of consciousness, but in fact, it is not. Given that this "gathering" has no existence apart from the mere accumulation and grouping together of those same particles and instants, and given that the individual items that are the basis of this "gathering" are not established as the self, it follows that the manifold aggregation of these same components is not the self either.

It might be thought that the self is something other than the three items previously mentioned (body, mind, and name). Once again, this is not the case. If it were, then the self would necessarily remain as a residue following the removal of each of the aggregates and so on. But this is refuted by direct perception: nothing remains to be found. Therefore, since the self and the aggregates are neither the same nor different, it is impossible for them to belong to each other or to subsist in the manner of a support and something supported. For example, axle, shafts, wheels, and so on, when gathered together, are called a "chariot." And yet if one investigates correctly, the chariot has absolutely no existence either as those items or as something separate from them. It is a mere designation. In fact, the "chariot" and the "parts" are completely unconnected.

One might well ask, "Why are beings deluded? What is it that makes them apprehend a self?" One can say only that it is because of a mistaken perception from beginningless time and through clinging to nonexistent things as if they were real—like mistaking a rope for a snake—that beings are deluded. Indeed, because the rope is coiled and because it is dark, one's eyes may be deceived, and through thinking that the rope is a snake, one feels great fear and dread. However, when the mistake occurs, it is not as if the rope goes somewhere else and a snake arrives and takes its place. The rope is not the snake, but neither is it something separate from it. In truth, even though there is absolutely no connection between the rope and a snake, the impression that there is a snake there happens simply through mistaken perception. On the other hand, one has only to light a lamp so that everything becomes clearly visible and one will see the rope directly. And, having detected the rope's real features, one will be freed of any fear of the imagined snake. Once again, it is not that the previously absent rope comes back and that the previously present snake is expelled. For from the very beginning, there has never been any snake in the rope.

In just the same way, it is through the power of mistaken perception and belief that beings take the five aggregates to be the self and are thereby deceived. And yet, as it was said earlier, thanks to an investigation that goes to the vital point, the resulting state of complete certainty utterly overturns one's clinging to an "I." This happens through the removal of one's earlier misunderstanding. It is not as if some concrete self is now removed, for from the very first, the "I," or self, has never been seen to exist. It is simply not found.

The nonexistence of the personal self is the ultimate object of realization for the Śrāvakas. Thanks to their understanding that within the gathering of the five aggregates of their continuum, there is no inherently existent "I," or self, they are able to put an end to attachment and the other defilements engendered on the basis of the view of the transitory collection (*'jig tshogs la lta ba*).[20] On the other hand, since they do not completely realize the no-self of all phenomena—that is to say, their nature of equality (*mnyam nyid*),[21] they are unable to remove the conceptual veil, which consists in ascribing true existence to the three spheres [of agent, object, and action]. And it is because they fail to realize the equality of existence and peace, of samsara and nirvana, that they cannot escape the nirvana that is an extreme. This is the crux of the matter. When, however, they realize the state of equality, it will be impossible for them to fall into the extreme of nirvana, and they will understand how, in the last analysis, there is but a single vehicle.

The same is true for the self of phenomena. Because there is clinging to "I," the thought of, and attachment to, "my body," "my mind," "my name" arise. And the same applies, for the same reason, to the aggregates, elements, and sources[22]—all the phenomena of the universe and the beings it contains. When these are examined, one finds the same situation as was previously described.

Now the infinitesimal particles, the ultimate range of form, and the indivisible instants of consciousness are in fact no more than the imputations of philosophical speculation. They do not actually exist [as things in themselves]. For when one considers the indivisible, partless particles of which gross objects are [said to be] composed, they themselves can be further divided into parts, top, bottom, and so on. They become sixfold or tenfold [according to direction]—which, of course, disproves the assertion that they are partless. Moreover, if this were not the case, then no matter how many particles were assembled together, they would never occupy the space of more than one partless particle, and the construction of gross extended objects would be impossible. Even a heap of such particles would be no more than a single infinitesimal particle. Moreover, since the particles are all perfectly equal in size, there is no question of one such particle entering, or being contained within, another.

The situation is similar with the indivisible instants of consciousness, the ultimate range, or limit, of the mind. When these instants form a continuity, every instant has an earlier and a later part, and consequently a central part. If this were not the case, it would be impossible for the instants to form a continuity, with the result that an entire kalpa would be no more than a single instant.

Therefore, since [the particles of] matter and [the instants of] consciousness cannot be found, nonassociated conditioning factors, such as names, are merely labels attached to particular situations in which mind and matter are brought together. They have no existence apart from this.

Being included within these three items [form, mind, and name], all conditioned or compounded things (Skt. *saṃskṛta*, Tib. *'dus byas*)[23] are therefore completely unreal. They do not exist except as mere designations devised in contrast with unconditioned things, which are their opposites. They have no existence in fact. All phenomena, therefore, be they conditioned or unconditioned, have a purely nominal existence as names and nothing more. They are without the slightest degree of intrinsic being. They cannot be found.

Names, moreover, are just labels. As indicators of meaning established at some time in the past, they can always be newly attached in all manner of ways [to other things] according to time and place. There is no intrinsic connection between names and the things they designate. Moreover, if one analyzes a name down to its limit or final constituents, it cannot go beyond the individual syllables or sounds of which it is composed, and these, when investigated, do not exist inherently. Thus one can say that when things are analyzed to their limit, there is only dharmatā. When thoughts are analyzed to their limit, there is a state of no thought. When speech is analyzed to its limit, there is no speech. All of them—things, thoughts, and speech—are but the state of equality.

So why, one may well ask, do all these things appear? The answer is that they do so by way of dependent arising. And it is precisely because the nature of dependent arising is emptiness that they are able to appear. If this were not so, if phenomena were established as truly existent on the ultimate level, they could not be mutually dependent and the entire sequence of causes and effects would be severed.

Consequently, all the phenomena that now appear are, from the very moment of their being perceived, without the slightest degree of inherent being. *Form*[24] and so on *is emptiness*. But without ever stirring from their ultimately empty nature, the whole variety of things unceasingly appears. *Emptiness is form* and so on. And since emptiness is not found anywhere apart from appearance; and since appearance is not found anywhere apart from emptiness, *emptiness is none other than form* and so on, and *form* and so on *is none other than emptiness*. So it is that the primordial, inseparable union of appearance and emptiness, the state of great equality, the dharmatā beyond all conceptual construction, is the fundamental and final nature of all phenomena.

Now, depending on whether or not the union of appearance and emptiness is realized as it is, there occurs either the perception of enlightened beings (in which the nature and the appearance of phenomena are in harmony) or the deluded perceptions of samsara (in which phenomena do not appear in the way that they truly are). Furthermore, according to valid cognition on the conventional level, the perceptions of phenomena are classified as twofold: as either pure or impure; and it is thanks to this that we are able to speak of samsara and nirvana, of bondage and liberation, and so on, positing without confusion all the categories of the ground, path, and result. By contrast, from the standpoint of final realization, no distinction is made in the nature of these things, and this constitutes their single, ultimate truth, their state of equality.

When one is able to realize and become habituated to this state of equality (the final nature of things beyond increase and decrease), the cognitive subject—the mind, or consciousness—also subsides within that same state. And the dualistic perception of appearance and emptiness, existence and nonexistence—that is to say, cognition in terms of apprehending subject and an apprehended object[25]—will no longer be possible.

As it is said,

> When something and its nonexistence
> Both are absent from before the mind,
> No other option does the latter have:
> It comes to perfect rest, from concepts free.[26]

The meditative equipoise of the Āryas, in which such conceptual construction has subsided in the ultimate expanse, can in no way be envisaged in ordinary terms of this or that. As it is said,

> Beyond thought or word or formulation is the prajñāpāramitā.

And,

> The ultimate is not within the reach of intellect.
> For intellect is said to be the relative.[27]

This fundamental nature beyond the ordinary mind is utterly free of defects to be dispelled and qualities to be gained. Therefore, there is nothing to be asserted or negated with regard to it, and nothing to be hoped for. As it is written in the *Sutra of the Non-arising of Phenomena*,[28]

> Enlightenment, it's said, is beings' nature.
> The nature of enlightenment is every being.
> Beings and enlightenment are not two different things.
> Sublimely great are those who realize this.

And as various sutras and tantras proclaim, for example, the *Sutra of the Precious Space* and the *Red Bhairava Tantra*,[29]

> Therein is nothing to remove
> And thereto not the slightest thing to add.
> The perfect truth viewed perfectly
> And perfectly beheld is liberation.

When things are said to be "without intrinsic being" or described as "unborn and unceasing," these are just ascriptions made by the ordinary mind. They are no more than a point of entry into the final ultimate truth. Such ideas are not the actual ultimate in itself but are referred to as the *figurative* or *concordant ultimate*, for they are no more than the object of the ordinary intellect. The final, nonfigurative ultimate, the union [of appearance and emptiness] is free of every conventional category—of subject and object, of thought and word. In being empty, free of characteristics, and beyond expectation,[30] the ultimate truth in itself has the nature of luminosity; it is the sphere of the deep, primordial wisdom of the meditation of the Āryas. As we find in the sutra,[31]

> Deep and peaceful, thought-free, luminous, unmade:
> The nectar-truth, this now I have discovered.
> Were I to teach it, none would understand;
> And so I will remain, not speaking, in the forest.

Suchness is ineffable, beyond the path of speech.
The nature of phenomena resembles space.
All mind, all movement of the intellect, is gone—one knows
The ultimate, the great, the wondrous utterly supreme.

When this union [of appearance and emptiness], beyond all conceptual constructs, is made into a mental object and thought about, the ordinary mind, the subject, meditates on it in the manner of a general idea or mental image; and this is the path of the sutras. Once this state of union, the absence of conceptual construction, is established on the basis of the ordinary mind, the authentic ultimate truth is meditated upon; and this is the swift path of the Mantrayāna.

But how does this happen? All outer and inner phenomena, the external universe and the beings it contains, appear in the mind; they manifest by virtue of the mind, which is the root of all things. It is therefore impossible for there to be any concrete thing truly existing separate and apart from the mind. Everything is like the appearances of a dream. When one is asleep, one might—depending on one's habits—dream of horses, or oxen, and so on. The things that one dreams of had no existence before one fell asleep; neither will they exist after one has woken up. And in the meantime, they are no more than appearances occurring in a deluded mind. Dream horses, dream oxen, dream places, and so on have not the slightest trace of intrinsic being. In the same way, the places, mental states, and bodies, which endlessly appear within our present waking state, had no existence previously—before there was any deluded straying from the primordial state; and they will not exist in the future when delusion dissolves in the ultimate expanse. It is only now, and for the deluded mind, that they appear to exist even though they do not exist in truth. They are like the black lines appearing before the eyes of someone who has eaten *dhatura*.[32]

Now, since this hallucinatory, extramental world, which appears on the conventional level, is not the mind itself, and since it does not exist to the slightest degree as other than the mind, it is an empty form, appearing yet without existence. In the ultimate truth, appearance and emptiness cannot be distinguished, appearance and emptiness are inseparable. If one understands in this way, the position of the Cittamātra school, to the effect that outer objects have no inherent existence, is established.

But then one must observe one's inner consciousness, examining how mental states arise, remain, and depart. At first, one finds no place of origin and no mind that originates; the mind is empty. Then one finds that there is no place of remaining and no mind that remains; the mind is empty. Finally, there is no place of cessation and no mind that ceases; therefore the mind is empty. Although the mind cannot be identified as something with shape or color, it is, nevertheless, the basis for the endless emergence of the whole range of phenomenal appearance. In the very moment that phenomena appear, their nature is not other than emptiness. And since the unceasing radiance of emptiness manifests as phenomena in all their variety, appearance and emptiness are from the very outset inseparably united. When all the misconceptions regarding the mind are eliminated, as happens when one realizes the fourfold emptiness,[33] *the ground*—the Madhyamaka view of freedom from conceptual elaboration—is realized.

As one rests naturally and without any contrivance, without any distraction and without [purposefully] meditating, in the mind's fundamental nature, in which appearance and emptiness are inseparably united, one will come to the realization that the mind's stillness and movement have the same undivided nature. It is the very nature of the mind, luminous and empty, naked and uncontrived: it is coemergent, primordial wisdom. Because appearances and the mind are inseparable, as in the example of the water and the moon reflected therein, when manifold phenomena are understood to have the same taste, *the path*—the meditation of Mahāmudrā—is accomplished.

Then one watches this uncontrived, fundamental nature (the indivisible union of luminosity and emptiness). When the state of great equality (where neither appearance nor awareness is identified as such) is determined—not as some kind of inert object but as primordial purity, unborn, aware, and empty—this is the *result*, the primordial state of openness and freedom. It is the realization of the Great Perfection practice of "cutting through" (*trekchö*).

In the preceding views [of Cittamātra, Madhyamaka, and Mahāmudrā), the mind is objectified, and once [its nature] is decided, meditation follows accordingly. Thus a subtle analytical reasoning has taken place. In the Great Perfection, by contrast, when one comes to the clear conclusion that the nature of the mind, or awareness, is unborn, one comes directly onto it and consequently there is not much room for intellectual activity and deviation from the fundamental nature.

This is why Longchenpa, the omniscient King of Dharma, and the vidyādhara Terdak Lingpa and others expounded two methods. They said that, as the preliminary practice, the house of the ordinary mind should be destroyed. As the main practice, at the introduction to the nature of the mind, they said that one should come to a decisive conclusion that ultimate reality, the dharmatā, is awareness, empty and unborn. In the tantras and texts of the Great Perfection, there is extensive teaching on how the [ordinary] mind is to be distinguished from awareness.[34] However, the most essential key points are to be found in the oral teachings of my own glorious master.[35]

When this mind in its present immediacy, namely, awareness, is left just as it is without any alteration, this constitutes the "fourth state," in which all mental activity related to the three times—past, present, and future—subsides (*bzhi cha gsum bral*). It is a state in which appearance and mind are not identified as such, a state that is free of characteristics and cannot be pointed out. But this has to be resolved beyond doubt from within oneself. And when it is so resolved, that which is resolved and the resolving agent are not two [different things]. This is [what is called] "dharmatā," the state of great equality. What is meant by *dharmatā*? Its nature (*ngo bo*) is emptiness; it cannot be observed. Its character (*rang bzhin*) is luminosity present of itself. Its cognitive power (*thugs rje*) is all-embracing and unceasing. It is awareness, in which the three kāyas are not separate. In brief, the actual nature of the mind—this beginningless natural flow—is primordial awareness untouched by any alteration and contrivance.

Awareness may be indicated negatively (apophatically), by saying what it is not. It does not exist as an object of apprehension. It is not nonexistent as something annihilated. It is not the combination of these two together. Neither is it the negation of these two together. And beyond these last two alternatives, there is no other. Since awareness cannot be a conceptual object of focus, it cannot in any way be regarded as a thing.

Awareness can also be described positively (kataphatically) by explaining how it is experienced. It is utterly empty. It is completely clear and lucid. It is limpidly pure. It is evenly pervasive. It is a state of seamless openness.[36]

Awareness can also be indicated through analogies. Like space, it is without center or boundary. Like space-pervading sunlight, its luminosity is unconfined. In awareness, there is no inside and no outside; it is like a crystal ball. There is nothing within it that one might grasp; it is like the flight path of a bird. And again like space, it has no origin and no cessation. It is like a wish-fulfilling jewel, for every excellence is naturally complete in it. Unstained by fault or defect, it is like a lotus.

Warding off false opinions regarding these explanations, one can speak of awareness in the following terms. It is a great luminosity, unconfined, impartial; it is a great emptiness, inconceivable and unobservable; it is a great union, for the one is inseparable from the other. It is utterly beyond expression and the mind's conceiving; it is the great state beyond the ordinary mind.

As for the actual nature of awareness, it is ineffable, beyond verbal indication. It is inconceivable; no consciousness can know it. It is the great absence of conceptual construction; it is not found in any ontological extreme. And yet, because nothing is beyond awareness and everything is included in it, it can be meditated on.[37] It is self-cognizing awareness beyond verbal expression. It is the union of primordial purity and spontaneous presence, the sole sphere of self-arisen primordial wisdom. Awareness is endowed with many perfect qualities. Therefore, there is no effort and exertion in the practice and no expectation or fear with regard to the result. It is the immaculate, ultimate expanse, the sugatagarbha, emptiness endowed with supreme qualities.

In brief, the ordinary mind is agitated by movement of the karmic wind. Anything can arise within it, any kind of thought may occur to it in the form of ordinary [deluded] cognitions arising in terms of an apprehending subject and an apprehended object. By contrast, awareness—that is, self-arisen primordial wisdom, is the actual nature of this ordinary mind. It is itself unaltered by such dualistic subject-object cognitions. It is beyond thought, word, and formulation. It is the great state beyond the ordinary mind. Now, whether one relies on an investigation [of the mind] using Madhyamaka reasoning, such as the argument of "neither one nor many" (*gcig du bral*),[38] or whether one makes use of the pith instruction "the destruction of the house of the mind," as the preliminary practice, the same point is achieved. When emptiness is established through reasoned investigation, the [main] minds and mental factors[39] (which appear in chronological sequence and can be deconstructed and eliminated) are the defining characteristics of the conditioned mind. But whether it is examined or not, the nature of the mind, the realization of which is the result of such an investigation, is free of any arising and cessation throughout the three times. It is beyond all movement. Empty luminosity endowed with the essence of awareness is primordially beyond both bondage and freedom. When it is recognized directly, however much it may be investigated, it does not, to the slightest degree, move from its own nature, its way of being. This is the defining characteristic of ultimate reality, the unconditioned, uncompounded dharmatā. Such is the essential heart of the teaching of the sutras of definitive meaning and of the tantras.

This essence has been set forth at length with many words and expressions. In the second turning of the dharma wheel, it is defined as the fundamental nature endowed with the three doors of perfect liberation, as the absence of birth and cessation, and so on. In the third turning of the dharma wheel, it is defined as stable, peaceful, permanent, immovable, unchanging, and so on. In the mantra vehicle, it is the "causal tantra or continuum," the uncontrived mind; it is great bliss, self-arisen primordial wisdom, and so on. The ultimate essence thus expounded is the dharmatā itself, ultimate reality, the fundamental and unchanging nature [of all things]. Therefore, without getting tied up in what are but verbal expressions and without squandering one's energies in affirming or negating, one should skillfully make for the essential point. Rather than just imagining and pontificating about the primordial Buddha being the undeluded, all-knowing, all-perceiving, all-creating king, the enlightened mind, one should instead make a thorough investigation for oneself.

The true realization of this mind depends exclusively on the transfer of blessing power from the secret treasure of the master's wisdom. And this comes through the devotion that sees him or her as the buddha dharmakāya. A single word of a devoted prayer to the teacher is better than a hundred pointless investigations of the teachings on emptiness. Much speculation does indeed encourage the increase of the karmic wind. Therefore, from the very moment that the nature of awareness is unmistakenly introduced and recognized—through the blessing of one's teacher and the power of one's own meditation—one should drop all pointless activities that cause distraction and nakedly preserve the uncontrived nature of empty awareness that one has seen. This is imperative. In that situation, it is sometimes difficult to maintain the nature of awareness because it is spoiled by the "muddiness" of the contriving mind.[40] But if one remains firmly convinced that the root of all this [disturbance] is the unborn mind itself, any thoughts that arise from it, whether positive or negative, will neither help nor harm. There is no need to apply any other remedy. The thoughts will naturally subside, as when the knots into which a snake has been tied come loose all by themselves. The three ways in which thoughts subside will occur gradually,[41] thanks to one's practice. Consequently, no matter what thought arises—positive or negative—one's mind stream will not be trapped by it. Why so? Because the thought will not carry through into a second moment. And one is not trapped by a single instant of thought. The reason for this is that the first moment of thought is sealed, in the instant of its arising, by the realization of unborn and empty awareness. Just as in a golden land, where one cannot find ordinary stones even if one looks for them, likewise every thought has the nature of great and self-arisen primordial wisdom; it is not anything else to the slightest degree.

Consequently, for a practitioner who has accomplished the Great Perfection, there are no higher or lower vehicles, no swift or slow paths, no virtuous or nonvirtuous actions, and so on. There are no such qualitative differences. Everything is fully included, perfected, open and free, in the state of the single, self-arisen primordial wisdom. This is precisely why it is called *perfection*. And because the ground to be realized, the path to be traversed, and the result to be attained are none other than the self-arisen primordial wisdom, it is *great*. The meaning of the term *Great Perfection* is thus explained.

In this regard, certain persons of narrow outlook think that if the authentic ultimate truth is the sphere of meditative equipoise experienced by the Āryas (in which dualistic appearances do not occur), how can such a thing be actualized now, while one is an ordinary being [afflicted] with endless mental activity?

Generally speaking, all the paths of sutra and mantra are simply skillful methods whereby the ultimate truth, the state of great equality, the luminous dharmatā, may be directly or indirectly realized. And it cannot be denied that different practitioners either realize or fail to realize this depending on their varying abilities. Now the Secret Mantrayāna or Vajrayāna is designed chiefly for those of sharp capacity, and the essential instructions belonging to the two stages [of generation and perfection] introduce the nature of the mind as the dharmakāya. All these profound methods, in the tantras of both the New and Ancient translations, are nevertheless intended for beginners—that is, ordinary beings. The Āryas, who have attained the grounds of realization, have already realized the dharmatā and do not need to be introduced to the nature of their minds again.

In the Mahāyāna, which comprises the second and third turnings of the dharma wheel, the fundamental nature of the ground is extensively expounded as freedom from conceptual elaboration, the state of equality, the nature of luminosity, and so on. It was with this in mind that Sakya Pandita said in his *Distinguishing the Three Vows*,[42]

> If there is a view superior to the freedom
> From conceptual construction of the prajñāpāramitā,
> That view will be endowed with such construction.
> And if the view is free from this, there is no difference.[43]

Although the goal in both the sutra and the mantra vehicles is the dharmadhātu, that is, freedom from conceptual construction, the methods by which this is directly introduced in this very moment and then made into the path are concealed and not taught in the sutra path—which for this reason is limited in its range. By contrast, these methods are not hidden but are clearly and fully set forth in the Mantrayāna, which consequently knows no such limitation. Indeed, the Mantrayāna possesses many skillful means and is free of hardship.[44] Consequently, if the nature of the mind is introduced nakedly and directly to beginners of sharp capacity, they will be able to train and grow used to it in their actual experience.

The differences that divide the two vehicles—that which takes the cause, and that which takes the result, as the path—together with various ways of defining them are set forth extensively in texts such as the *Lamp of the Three Ways.*[45] For example, in the sutra of *The Instruction-Giving King,*[46] we find the following,

> Mañjuśrī then addressed the Teacher and said,
> "O Lord, you have most certainly affirmed
> Three vehicles of instruction.
> Yet why did you not speak about
> The vehicle of definitive instruction
> Where, fruit being naturally present in the cause,
> Buddhahood is not sought outside of oneself?"
> Answering him, the Teacher then declared,
> "For those who take an interest in the cause,
> I turned the wheel of teachings on that cause.
> The short path of the Vajrayāna
> Will appear in times to come."

In the same vein, the omniscient King of Dharma (Longchenpa) has said in his *Thunderous Melody of Brahma, the General Meaning of the Mantra Vehicle,*[47]

> The subject that already actualizes in this very moment
> the natural inseparability of the cause and result—
> namely, the primordial wisdom of great bliss, is the view
> of self-cognizing awareness, the view of direct experi-
> ence.[48] It is for this reason that the mantra vehicle is
> eminently superior to that of the sutras.

And as it is said in *The Vast Expanse,*[49]

> More important than primordial wisdom is defilement.
> For through the noose of fettering defilement,
> Self-arisen primal wisdom is discerned.
> Be convinced and understand that wisdom and defilement
> Are but one expanse, without duality.
> Have confidence; defilement will subside in its true nature.

But if one simply declares that the nature of one's present mind, the nakedly aware and empty state, is the primordial wisdom of the buddha dharmakāya, some beginners will not believe it. If, they will ask, the dharmakāya is the absence of conceptual construction (a state beyond dualistic perception) and if the nature of the contriving mind is precisely the domain of dualistic perception and characteristics, how can they possibly be one and the same? But these people are like simple children who have been told that a block of ice is just water. They do not believe it and ask how could it be so, when water is liquid and wet, while ice is as hard as stone.

Those who are in a slightly better situation, who rely on their own investigation and on teachings that they trust, will understand that the mind as they now experience it is deluded but that the nature of the mind, which emerges as the result of purification, is primordial wisdom. This is like thinking that even though water is not for the moment perceptible in ice, nevertheless, the latter's nature (emerging when the ice melts) is water—as though the ice were the [material] cause of the water.

Thanks, however, to the compassion of their teacher, their faith, their devotion, and so on, certain practitioners of sharp capacity are able to recognize directly the unborn nature of their present mind. Even though they do not yet realize that this is the nature of all phenomena, the omnipresent dharmadhātu—for such practitioners are not yet free of the obscuring veils to be abandoned on the path of seeing[50]—they are able nevertheless to grasp intellectually, prompted by the realization of the unborn nature of the mind, that all phenomena are unborn. They are like people who, having tasted a small fragment of ice, understand from then on that all ice is the same and will never again be mistaken in thinking that ice is not water. Now since such a realization is able to indicate or exemplify the primordial wisdom of the Āryas, it is called "example wisdom." And although such an understanding belongs to the temporary figurative ultimate (*gnas skabs rnam grangs pa'i don dam*), it is nevertheless far superior to one's previous understanding and experience [to the effect that ice is the material cause of water]. Indeed the difference between the first and second cases is like a drawing of the moon as compared with the reflection of the moon in water.

When, however, the ultimate, actual luminosity is realized, this is like the melting of the whole block of ice into water. When ice thaws, it does so gradually through the effect of fire or the sun; it does not turn into water all at once. In the same way, all the gross and subtle marks of dualistic perception, which form part of the obscurations to be abandoned on the path of meditation,[51] are exhausted gradually, dissolving into the expanse of the great equality of ultimate reality, or dharmatā. Finally, just as when the entire block of ice has melted [and no trace of the original ice is left], in the same way, not the slightest mark of dualistic perception will remain, and one will dwell permanently in the state of meditative equipoise. This is the very ground of the final state of enlightenment.

Now it is said that if the ground of buddhahood is examined, it has two aspects. First, the self-experience of a buddha—the kāya, the buddha field, and so on—manifests only within the radiance of the great equality of the dharmatā. For this reason, it does not at all exist as a dependently imputed phenomenon. Being entirely unconditioned and immaculate, it is the dharmakāya, the body of ultimate reality. Second, the relative and symbolic body of enlightenment (kun rdzob brda' yi sku) [that is, the form body, or rūpakāya] manifests from within the dharmakāya in the perception of others—namely, beings to be trained, as the unceasing magical display of dependent arising.

For this reason, when the form body of a buddha is seen to take birth and then to die, this is no more than a reflection of the limited capacity of the minds of beings to be trained. Likewise, when beings perceive the buddhas' knowledge of things in terms of a gradual process of cognition that sees knowledge objects in chronological sequence, this too occurs only because of the way in which phenomena appear on the conventional level. The truth is that since the objects of the buddhas' knowledge are without intrinsic being, they are a state of equality. Ultimately, in their fundamental nature, their ultimate reality, they transcend all movement and change. They are like space.

Now regarding the realization experienced by beings who are now on the path, there is first the fact that it arises, and then the question of its growth or decline. From the first ground onward, realization develops and does not diminish, whereas on the ground of buddhahood, realization neither increases nor decreases. For at that time, the four kinds of "grounds of abiding," such as the ground of abiding in the propensity to ignorance,[52] as described in the common vehicle; the obscurations that consist in the propensity to experience the three successive stages of light, increase of light, and complete culmination of light (*snang gsum 'pho ba'i bag chags*),[53] spoken of in the common mantra vehicle; and the movement of the impure wind-mind,[54] discussed in the uncommon vehicle of the Great Perfection—all such extremely subtle dependent arisings are exhausted or arrested in the ultimate expanse. It is then that the wisdom body of a buddha manifests. This is the vajra, or indestructible, body; the permanent body; the everlasting, unchanging body.[55] It is the body that is beyond all movement and change throughout the entire passage of time. It is the body of the fourth time;[56] the time of equality.

Therefore, although from the point of view of ultimate reality, or dharmatā, there is no movement or change, yet from the point of view of phenomenal manifestation, movement and change seem to occur. But because these are distinctions made by the contriving mind, it is important to differentiate understanding, experience, and realization. As the saying goes, "Understanding is like a patch—it will come off; experience is like mist—it will fade away; but realization is like the king of mountains—it will neither move nor change."

Therefore, regarding the discussion whether, for practitioners who are now on the path, periods of meditation and postmeditation are distinct or not, this should be understood in terms of the difference between experience and realization. The state of realization in which there is no difference between meditation and postmeditation occurs only on the level of perfect buddhahood and nowhere else. Indeed, it is taught that even for bodhisattvas on the three pure grounds, there is a postmeditation period. Now, when the nature of awareness is unmistakenly recognized through the paths of Mahāmudrā and the Great Perfection, many holy beings of the Mahāmudrā tradition and others believe that since awareness is experienced directly, this constitutes authentic ultimate luminosity. On the other hand, the omniscient Longchenpa and others say that in the true actualization of ultimate luminosity, twelve sets of one hundred excellent qualities,[57] among other things, must be present. Consequently, even though the awareness just referred to is experienced directly, Longchenpa and others identify it as the example luminosity.

These contrasting interpretations, however, are not in fact incompatible. For the former is expounded from the point of view of the fundamental nature of things, the dharmatā, while the latter is given from the standpoint of the appearing mode of phenomena. The proponents of the mind section of the Great Perfection belonging to the Zur tradition say that when one understands and recognizes one's present mind as being unborn, this [understanding and recognition] is part of the temporary figurative ultimate. For even though emptiness, the nature of things, has been truly realized, its qualities do not actually appear. And this is because the whole of phenomenal appearance has not subsided in the expanse of ultimate reality. As one trains progressively in emptiness, however, all hallucinatory phenomena will eventually subside, purified in the expanse of ultimate reality; it is then that every quality—right up to those on the ground of perfect buddhahood—will effortlessly appear. Therefore, even though there is no movement or change within the ultimate nature, it is quite correct to say that, from the standpoint of the practitioner on the path, there is a semblance of movement or change.

For practitioners on the path of accumulation, there is understanding; for those on the path of joining, there is experience; and for those on the path of seeing, there is realization. This has been affirmed by the great and noble beings who have well perceived the truth of the dharmatā, and it should be understood as a profound key point. Beginners, who are on the path of accumulation, rely on their teachers and listen to their instructions. Through an understanding that derives from study and reflection, they rid themselves of misconceptions regarding the fundamental nature of things—namely, the union [of appearance and emptiness]. When, on this basis, they recognize that the mind is unborn and have a decisive experience of this, the example luminosity arises in their mind stream. And since, thanks to the example luminosity, they will be directly joined to the ultimate luminosity, this stage is called the "path of joining." The occurrence or otherwise of the example luminosity is the criterion that determines whether one is on the path of joining or not. The moment when the example luminosity develops and transforms into ultimate luminosity is the point when the truth of ultimate reality, the dharmatā, is realized, and this is the path of seeing. From that moment onward, to grow used to what has been realized constitutes the path of meditation. And when this has been completed, the path of no more learning is attained.

Therefore, even in the case of the figurative ultimate, there are many distinctions in terms of the quality and speed of the path, depending on whether, by means of the profound methods, understanding and experience have occurred or not. Likewise, with regard to the way of seeing the ultimate directly, there are differences in terms of whether one sees it perfectly or not. For instance, when a sense object is seen, it is perceived perfectly or otherwise depending on whether it is seen closely or from afar. In the same way, there are considerable differences between the higher and lower stages of realization. And yet, although many statements are made regarding swift and slow paths and the presence or absence of differences once the noble ground of realization has been gained, this is not a matter of ordinary examination—necessarily so, for it is beyond discursive thought.

In short the common ground for the arising of all the phenomena of samsara and nirvana is ultimate reality, the dharmatā, the state of great equality. Since its nature is free of the eight conceptual extremes—arising and cessation, permanence and annihilation, coming and going, identity and difference—it is primordially pure. Because of its [luminous] character, it is not a nihilistic void. For the kāyas and wisdoms and all the qualities of buddhahood are primordially and naturally present in it, without their having to be sought elsewhere. Consequently, it is a state of the spontaneous presence [of the qualities of enlightenment]. Through the creative power of awareness, which is the union of luminosity and emptiness, all the phenomena of samsara and nirvana arise. The unceasing and unobstructed ground for their arising is all-embracing cognitive potency. These three aspects are referred to as nature, character, and cognitive potency, according to the conceptual aspects by which the dharmatā is indicated. But apart from that, they are not in the slightest way different. All phenomena of both samsara and nirvana are encompassed by all-embracing primordial wisdom, empty, luminous, and unceasing. And this is the ultimate nature, the dharmatā, of all phenomena, the state of great equality. It has never been, and will never be, a state of delusion. And even now, within the ground, delusion is not present. Dharmatā is the sole buddha dharmakāya, which is primordially free of delusion.

So it is that self-arisen primordial wisdom has not emerged from any cause; neither has it been generated by conditions. It depends on neither words nor the ascertainment of the mind. For this reason, the teachings speak of buddhahood that does not derive from the ordinary mind, of a result that derives from no cause, and of an instruction that derives from no transmission. If this self-arisen primordial wisdom is realized and experienced, one has reached the depth of all things. As it is said in the tantra *The Wheel of Self-Arisen Bliss*,[58]

> I found an enlightenment that came not from my mind.
> I realized a result that came not from a cause.

I know all instructions not deriving from transmission.
All the teachings of nine vehicles are but a single teaching.
Five poisons are all pure as the state beyond all sorrow.
The dharmakāya bursts forth from the vast expanse of
      Mind.

Ultimate reality, the dharmatā, can never be spoiled by the defects of ephemeral characteristics, such as arising and so on. Therefore, it is by nature stable, peaceful, unmoving, everlasting, and thus it is ever-youthful. Although at the moment, it is enveloped in the vaselike snare of the moving karmic wind, the root of the defiled mind, nevertheless every unsurpassed excellence, such as the [ten] strengths,[59] is naturally present in it, like a body enclosed within a vase, for which reason, it is called the "ever-youthful vase body."

Its display [that is, the appearances of the ground] manifests in various ways. Since it arises as cognitive potency, compassion for beings appears. Since it arises as light, there manifests the radiance of the five primordial wisdoms. Since it arises as primordial wisdom, there occurs an indwelling wisdom that purifies the mind's defilements. Since it arises as the enlightened bodies, there manifest the deities of limpid luminosity. Since it arises in a nondual manner, there is no apprehension of identity or difference. Since it arises in a manner free from all extreme ontological positions, there is freedom in the one and only sphere—the perfect ground that is beyond movement and change. Since it arises as pure primordial wisdom, the appearances of nirvana are unceasing. Since it arises as impure samsara, the hallucinatory appearances of the six classes of beings occur in the manner of magical illusions. And since the ground for the arising of these eight doors, or ways,[60] is unobstructed, it is called the "dimension of the spontaneous presence of the ground." These eight ways of arising refer to the display of the ground's appearance. This display has no directional location. Since it is the experience of self-cognizing awareness, it is coexistent with it. The difference between buddhas and beings lies simply in the recognition or nonrecognition of this. For awareness is the sole cause of both samsara and nirvana, which are like the front and back of a single hand.

When the ground's appearances arise within the primordial ground, this self-experience of that same ground, the dharmatā, does not involve any delusion. But since through coemergent ignorance, acting as the cause, there is a failure to recognize the nature of this appearance, and since conceptual ignorance, acting as the condition, imputes "self" and "other" as separate, the dualistic cognitions of apprehender and apprehended grow increasingly coarse. So it is that beings are caught in the trap of adventitious delusion. Endless appearances arise [subjectively] in terms of thought, word, and deed, or [objectively] in terms of an environment and the minds and bodies [of beings]; and all of them veil the face of the ground, or ultimate reality. No need to talk about the manifest realization of the qualities of the ground, one does not even know that they are dwelling in oneself. This is due to the particular obscurations of every individual being from the point of view of the hallucinatory mode of appearance. From the standpoint of the fundamental nature of phenomena, however, since there is never any stirring from the original condition of the ground, the dharmatā, it follows that all phenomena, which are pervaded by it, are the ground's appearances. They are none other than the display of primordial wisdom. Appearances *are* the enlightened body; sounds *are* enlightened speech; and all mental processes *are* the enlightened mind. One's body, speech, and mind are primordially the three vajras; and all appearances and activities are nothing but the three mandalas. If one can take them as the path and experience them without discarding or adding anything, without rejecting or adopting anything, all the stains of impure delusion will be naturally purified and cleared away. It is just as when one wakes and one's dreams vanish. All appearances and activities will arise as the kāyas and primordial wisdoms.

In the same way, beings are at first deluded with regard to the appearances of the ground and are at the present moment dwelling in delusion. But because the appearances of the ground arise within the ground, the state of great equality, when beings die and the process of elemental dissolution comes to an end, all the eighty states of mind[61] come gradually to a halt, and beings remain for a moment in the ground, the dharmatā.

For this reason, the three dimensions—"outer," "inner," and "other"—are blended together. This refers to the birth and destruction of the outwardly manifesting world and its inhabitants, the fluctuations of the inwardly manifesting wind-mind of the body, and the "other" dimension—namely, the generation stage of the support and supported (the palace and the deities) and their dissolution into luminosity (in the perfection stage). And in this context, one should understand that the factors to be purified, the agents of purification, and the ground and result [of purification] are all inseparable. This constitutes the ultimate realization of the unsurpassed tantras of the great secret.

The two doors of freedom and delusion spoken of in the uncommon tradition of the Great Perfection, which are present when the appearances of the ground arise within the primordial ground, and the possibility of freedom or delusion at the moment of death, or in the bardo, as happens in our present situation, thus amount to the same thing. In the latter case, when the luminosity at the moment of death and the appearances of the bardo of ultimate reality manifest in succession, practitioners may gain freedom, according to their varying capacities, either in the dharmakāya at the moment of death or in the sambhogakāya while in the bardo state. Ordinary beings, on the other hand, fail to recognize this luminosity and are alarmed by sounds, lights, rays, and so on. Their minds are veiled by the dualistic cognitions of the apprehended and the apprehender, and it is thus that their mental bodies in the hallucinatory bardo are produced.

While one is practicing on the path, various experiences show that if one clings outwardly to the appearances of the six consciousnesses, inwardly to the thoughts of the five poisons, and secretly to the fundamental nature of one's mind as things to be adopted or rejected, one is fettered. If, on the other hand, one leaves all these things just as they are—and this is the crucial point—one is free. Finally, when the path of trekchö is fully accomplished, and the body is on the point of dissolving into atoms, one is able effortlessly to display emanations and transformations such as the ten limitless *āyatanas*,[62] which are the appearing aspect of the limpid wind-mind. Moreover, the visions and so forth on the path of thögal are effortlessly generated thanks to the fact that the radiance of the ground luminosity is mingled with the subtle wind-mind. Since all true paths[63] are mixed with conditioned aspects, they develop or diminish in succession. Finally, however, this display dissolves into the ground, the inner expanse of primordial purity, and manifest enlightenment occurs in the place of freedom,[64] the original primordial purity. The Primordial Lord, the first Buddha, is free, having entered the original, primal expanse of the ground where there has never been any delusion. This is the reason for his name. And so it is said, "There is no first and last Buddha." And also, "I am the first Buddha."

There is no turning back [from the place of freedom], for the fundamental nature of the ground, ultimate reality, has been actualized exactly as it is. The state of delusion that has veiled its mode of appearance, together with all habitual tendencies, has gone forever. Just as when a seed is burned by fire, or when one is cured of smallpox, what is gone can never return, for the final transformation has taken place.

Those who wish to practice upon this profound path should understand that everything that is pervaded by the ground, the dharmatā, is simply the display of primordial wisdom, the appearance of the ground. Without affirming or negating, and without clinging to anything, they should recognize awareness, all-pervading and unceasing—the empty but luminous state of equality, the ground, the dharmatā. And they should do this by leaving it unaltered and uncontrived, seeing it nakedly in its great and primordial openness and freedom. Subsequently, they should perfect this skill and finally achieve stability in it. This is a point of the highest importance.

A Ho

In the sugatagarbha, luminosity of the primordial ground's
　　expanse,
There is no trace of dual appearance.
There is no thought "samsara and nirvana."
But when the appearances of the ground, spontaneously arrayed,
Unfold in outward-spreading luminosity,
The doors of freedom and delusion adventitiously arise.
Because Samantabhadra saw this play of primal wisdom,
His self-experience, as his own display,
He crushed the seed of coemergent ignorance abiding in the
　　ground.[65]
While he, the first born, reached
The place of freedom, pure from the beginning,
By us is this existence made, through forgeries of ignorance.
And yet, like gold beneath the earth, like flame within a vase,
The buddha element, the dharmatā, the wisdom all-pervading,
Empty and yet luminous, beyond all change throughout the
　　triple time,
Dwells naturally within us.
There is no need, therefore, for sorrow or dejection.
You should concentrate on practice.
The fruit of training for a myriad ages on the paths of arduous
　　vehicles,
The wisdom that abides within,
Is plainly manifest upon the short path of the Ati yoga.
When by your own strength you embark
Upon the supreme vehicle that's free of all travail,
The time has come to follow in the footsteps
Of thousands of vidyādharas of times gone by.
Climb up upon the stallion of revulsion for samsara's devil-
　　haunted land.
Whipped forward by determination to be free,
And on the wings of diligence's wind,

Ride swiftly through the sky of skillful means and wisdom.
For if you are not quickly gone, the time will never come
For liberation from the jail of threefold suffering.
You should trust in karma, law of cause and fruit—
It is the stair to higher destinies.
The sincere resolve to leave samsara is the gateway to the path of
    freedom.
Sincere refuge in the Three Jewels is the hallmark of a Buddhist.
Without these three, there is no other way;
Be at all times diligent in practice!
Bodhichitta for the sake of others is the royal road of the
    bodhisattvas.
The union of view and action is what brings omniscience.
If all these are not linked with sublime, primal wisdom,
How can they become the path of true, authentic Mahāyāna?
If the seeds of the four kāyas are not moistened
With the nectar of four ripening empowerments,
If the stem and fruit of generation and perfection do not grow,
With skill in perfect, pure samaya,
The claim to enter Mantrayāna is just a painted flame.
If, most especially, the empowering blessing of the wisdom
    lineage
Does not through your devotion, penetrate your hearts,
You hear the dry words of repeated explanation—
You wander like a person blind from birth
Even when indwelling wisdom is directly shown.
But if you actually see your teacher truly as a buddha
And have the fortune to imbibe the nectar of profound instruction
With the cup of threefold faith,
Then like blind men who get their sight again,
Will it be hard for you to actualize, through blessings' power,
The primal wisdom dwelling in your minds?
You will not be deceived by dark and dull blank states of mind,
Or led astray by individual experiences of emptiness and
    luminosity.

Free of all conceptual targets, the unclouded sun of confidence
Will rise up from within—the special treasure of the practice
   lineage.
All phenomenal existence, all samsara and nirvana, are but
   mind's display.
And yet if "mind" is looked for, it is nowhere to be found.
It's something that was never born.
Appearances and mind cannot be parted,
They are like the water and the moon reflected there.
Happy are the yogis who have understood
That all things thus have but a single taste.
Within the vast expanse—the first, fresh openness,
The freedom of awareness, the space primordially pure
That's free of all conceptual constructs—
There, spontaneously present,
Are appearances that never cease
Of luminous primordial wisdom,
The all-pervading cognitive potential of awareness
That is the source of everything.
Such is the fundamental state wherein—how wonderful!—
The triple kāya is beyond all separation.
Its nature, from the very first, is empty;
It therefore does not dwell in the extreme of permanence.
Its character is luminous;
It therefore does not touch the extreme of annihilation.
Although of these two aspects we now speak,
They are not two but equal.
And in this space of evenness,
All phenomena of both samsara and nirvana
Are discovered (there's no need to seek them),
Totally, primordially, present.
Deluded are the ones who take to be existent what does not exist.
How tiring thus to build a dam for water of a mirage!
What point is there in taking up the arduous burden of so many
   hardships?

If you reach the essential point of how things are,
Bondage, liberation—these are not two things.
If you reach this space of evenness,
You have attained the utter peak of view and meditation.
The hundred fetters of contrived philosophy subside all by
    themselves.
Appearances are none other than the play of great primordial
    wisdom.
There is no need for taking or rejecting;
No need is there for purposeful fixating.
Disregard them! Give them up!
Without an understanding of this crucial point,
Experiencing as separate emptiness and luminosity,
Some fools mistake the nature of awareness of the Great
    Perfection.
Wind-energy disturbs their mental sight, their minds are clogged
    by thoughts,
And finally their life-wind will itself be troubled.
What use is there in all this toil?
Many take as their main meditation
The simple absence of all thought.
They pass their human lives in blank and thoughtless states.
Devoid of any clear, decisive view,
They lay the ground for their despair.
They run great risk of wasting all their freedoms and advantages.
Some are tricked by the experience of a single-pointed
    concentration.
They claim their nights and days are spent
In seamless luminosity without the need for meditation.
And yet, when troubles come,
They act like ordinary people.
They vie with others in their practice.
What benefit is there in such behavior?
All such acts of the contriving mind
Just show the movements of the karmic wind.

Reject them. Let them go without a care.
Instead, just keep the nature of awareness of whatever comes.
Leave it uncontrived and fresh.
Small will be your errors and mistakes!

The garland of this song
Is just as it arose unprompted in my mind.
I, Padma Vijaya, beloved son of mighty teachers,
To help my vajra brethren of one mind with me,
Sang this as it came to mind, devoid of hope and fear.

Mangalam

2

An Instruction for
Khenpo Jigme Drayang

Namo Guru Buddha Dharmakāyaya!

Khenpo Jigme Drayang[66] has said that he needs an explanation of
how to maintain the practice and how to act in the postmeditation
period—even though, of course, he knows all the general ways of
traversing the path and of preserving the practice in both a meditative session and in the postmeditation periods, as described in the
scriptures of the sutras and tantras.

All these methods have the same radical purpose: to act as
much as possible as an antidote to ego-clinging and defilement.
On the path of the sutras, the understanding that extramental
objects are devoid of true existence brings to an end the mental
attitude of clinging to them as real. To be more precise, on the
basis of an object of desire—a beautiful woman, for example—the
intellect (the cause of defective mental activity) gives rise to desire.
When this happens, one may apply an antidote by examining this
[seemingly] extramental object (the woman) and meditate on her
unattractive aspects. Or again, one may train oneself in the understanding of her illusory nature by meditating on the fact that she
is empty of true existence. These are the only paths or methods set
forth. At this level, there is no exposition of the crucial point of the
path whereby desire or aversion spontaneously subsides in awareness[67] (objectless and self-illuminating). The two earlier methods
are therefore referred to as the "long path" and can be compared to

a dog chasing after a stone [rather than the person who threw the stone]. Since this method does not use ordinary defilement as the path itself, it exhibits a certain lack of knowledge, or limitation, on the level of skillful means.

In the Mantrayāna generally and particularly in the case of the extraordinary and unsurpassed teachings of Mahāmudrā and the Great Perfection, once it has been established that appearances are the mind, that the mind is emptiness, that emptiness means the absence of conceptual construction, that the absence of conceptual construction is the state of union [of appearance and emptiness], and that the state of union is inexpressible or beyond the ordinary mind, defilements may be used directly as the path. This therefore is an eminently superior approach. It may be compared with the lion that chases [not the stone itself] but the one who threw the stone. Accordingly, it is through recognizing defilements as primordial wisdom, suffering as great bliss, and samsara as nirvana, that one is able to use defilements as the path. This approach has no limit on the level of skillful means, it is free of difficulties, and so on.[68] Thanks to these special features, it is a swift path; and yet, in truth, the only difference between these two approaches simply consists in whether one looks outward or inward. It should be understood, however, that if one fails actually to apply this second approach to one's own mind, simply knowing about it will be of no help. And if one slips into the attitude of looking outward, it is no different from the other methods.

Now there are some slight differences between Mahāmudrā and Dzogchen, depending on whether one says that appearances are or are not the mind, or whether the perceived appearance and the appearing object are the same or not, and so on. They are different too in the way that, on the one hand, the ordinary mind is distinguished from the nature of the mind and, on the other, the ordinary mind is distinguished from awareness. Nevertheless, apart from these small but subtle differences of expression, it should be understood that there is no conflict between Mahāmudrā and

Dzogchen. They are equal in touching the crucial point: the realization of the truth of the dharmatā.

As to the question whether appearances are or are not the mind, and whether one can distinguish between a perceived appearance and an object that appears, I will not, in the present context, discuss the assertions and arguments of the great texts of the Vaibhāṣika, Sautrāntika, Madhyamaka, Cittamātra, and other tenet systems. Regarding the traditions of Mahāmudrā and the Great Perfection, however, the lord Gotsangpa[69] affirms (on the Mahāmudrā side), "It is said that whatever appears to one's own mind is one's mind; but what appears to others is not so." On the other hand, in the Great Perfection, the omniscient Longchenpa has said, "Appearance as perceived is the mind, but the appearing object is not the mind." Both these statements come to the same point. The external thing, the object that appears commonly to all, does so through the power of habitual tendencies and is without true existence. It is like the falling hairs [seen by those with an optical disorder] or the visions of a dream. The external object, therefore, does not exist in the slightest way either as the mind or as something different from the mind. As we find in the *Introduction to the Middle Way*,

> The vast array of sentient life,
> The varied universe containing it, is formed by mind.
> The Buddha said that wandering beings are from karma
>   born.
> Dispense with mind and karma is no more.[70]

And it is said in one of the sutras,

> Various bodies and possessions,
> Experiences of joy and sorrow
> Are the mind's projections; they are made by mind.
> By way of an example, they are like dreams.

Accordingly, things appearing in the common consensus are the manifestations, in the form of external objects, of the habitual tendencies produced by the same kind of actions performed by all and imprinted on the mind, or rather the universal ground. In truth, however, there are no external, concrete objects actually existing in and of themselves in the common consensus. Things are to be understood more in terms of the "water" that manifests differently according to pure or impure karmic perception [in the different realms of beings].[71] The contention that what appears to us is not different from our own mind will be addressed in due course.

Likewise, the difference between the ordinary mind and the nature of the mind, and between the ordinary mind and awareness comes to the same essential point. According to Mahāmudrā, all the minds and mental factors occurring in the three worlds partake of the ignorant and deluded mind, the ground that contains the habitual tendencies of samsara. Its ultimate condition, the undeluded fundamental state or the pure innate nature of the mind, is said, in the Mahāmudrā teachings, to be the dharmakāya. In the Great Perfection, on the other hand, the deluded mind, ignorant of its own nature, together with its dualistic (apprehender-apprehended) cognitions, is labeled "mind," whereas primordial wisdom, which knows its own nature—the unconditioned state of the inseparable union [of appearance and emptiness]—is called and introduced as "awareness." There is no conflict at all between these two approaches [of Mahāmudrā and Dzogchen].

If one does not succeed, through study and reflection, in removing all misconceptions concerning the profound meaning, the fundamental nature of phenomena, or if one has not had a decisively effective experience of this fundamental nature through the reception of the teacher's blessing, then no matter how Madhyamaka, Mahāmudrā, and Dzogchen are explained, they will be of no benefit. For these explanations go no further than an intellectual view and do not become the authentic path. If, on the other hand, one understands correctly and has profound certainty, unfettered by doubt, with regard to this true and fundamental nature, one will not depreciate Madhyamaka and Mahāmudrā—preferring the Great Perfection as something superior to them, for in their very nature they are all equal. Moreover, all vehicles, starting from the most inferior eternalist and nihilist views of the non-Buddhist schools and going right up to the highest view of Ati yoga, are the expression of the one and only self-arisen primordial wisdom. This is to say that they are all perfectly included within it. And this is why—using the words in their literal sense—one speaks of this wisdom's "great perfection." One should understand, however, that to entangle oneself in the fetters of the views and meditations— described in intellectual terms in the tenet systems—is to create nothing but difficulty for oneself, like silkworms trapping themselves in cocoons of their own silk.

Regarding the implementation of the actual practice on the path, there is, generally speaking, the analytical meditation of the *panditas* and the resting meditation of the *kusāli* yogis."[72] These two paths are taught according to the mental aptitude of the practitioner concerned. For those who require an analytical approach, the various philosophical propositions regarding manifest and hidden objects and the existence or nonexistence of the self-cognizing mind, all are expounded in the great textual traditions, together with the four or five great Madhyamaka arguments,[73] such as the argument of neither one nor many. In the case of practitioners like ourselves, however, the essential points should be grasped according to the pith instructions of our teachers. And these are as follows.

No matter how the objects of the six consciousnesses appear— whether in terms of objects of desire, such as sexual partners, or objects of resentment, such as enemies—they are all, good or bad, to be understood as aspects of the mind. Indeed, if the aspects of the objects in question did not appear in the mind, there would be no evidence of their existence, and they would be powerless to produce reactions of desire or anger, or to act as the source of benefit or harm. We would all be like the inhabitants of Uttarakuru![74] It is because beings cling to what appears in their mind as something to be accepted or rejected that they engage in action and wander in samsara. But if they were to perceive these appearances as neither good nor bad, and if they did not cling to them as such, mere appearances would neither help nor harm them.

As it is said,

> We will not refute the mere appearance;
> But just refrain from thinking it exists in truth.[75]

And as Tilopa said to Naropa,[76]

> Clinging, not appearance, fetters you.
> Therefore, cut your clinging, Naropa.

The great master of Oddiyana, moreover, explained the crucial point of using the six consciousnesses as the path in the instruction "What appear as objects for your eyes . . ." and so on. It should be understood that all these quotations convey the same essential message.

Therefore, even when beings fall down into the hell realms and suffer the torments of heat and cold, it is simply their mind appearing in the aspect of pain. For if these experiences did not appear in the mind, who or what would know about such heat or cold, or about the guardians of hell and so on? And when one attains the fruit of buddhahood, it is in just the same way that the kāyas, buddha fields, qualities of primordial wisdom, enlightened activities, and so on are no more than what appears in the utterly pure mind. They have no existence apart from it. Likewise, it is said that the field of Shakyamuni, the buddha of our time, appears differently according to the purity or impurity of our own mind.[77]

Therefore, all appearances, pure and impure, of friends and enemies and of all the suffering and happiness of this present time—which are the objects of our clinging, of our acceptance or rejection—are mere appearances occurring in our mind. They have no existence apart from it, in just the same way that the reflection of the moon is not separate from the water in which it appears.

Therefore, whatever arises, whatever appears in the mind—joy, sorrow, and so forth—none of it exists as a substantial entity separate from the mind itself. Indeed, if it existed as an entity different from the mind, it would be impossible ever to experience it. Neither would there be any means of bringing it to an end. It could not be stopped. If the mind, the basis of all appearance, is examined, it will be found to transcend the three stages of arising, remaining, and ceasing, as these unfold in chronological sequence. The nature of the mind is empty, and this emptiness is not an emptiness contrived anew. It is the primordially subsisting emptiness of the expanse of ultimate reality, free from all characteristics and conceptual construction. But the naturally unconditioned nature of mind, freedom from conceptual construction, emptiness, is not some kind of unilaterally inert and space-like void—a complete nonentity like the child of a barren woman. On the contrary, by its very nature it knows everything and is aware of everything. It is self-cognizing and self-illuminating. And the expression of this emptiness can arise as anything at all. If this were not the case, how would it be possible for the mind of a perfectly enlightened buddha to arise—the primordial wisdom that knows all things in their nature and in their multiplicity? Thus, the nature of the mind is the inseparable union of appearance and emptiness, luminosity and emptiness, awareness and emptiness. It is ineffable and beyond the ordinary intellect. It is great primordial wisdom, the fourth time, the time of equality.[78]

If with this understanding one examines well, both a divinely beautiful woman (an object of desire) and the murderer who killed one's own father (an object of hate) are appearances in one's mind; they do not exist otherwise. Now the basis for the appearance of these two phenomena is the mind itself, the mind's fundamental nature, the state of union (of appearance and emptiness), the freedom from conceptual construction, emptiness itself. And for this reason, not the slightest thing, good or bad, done by either the woman or the murderer can be found. For they are like paints that cannot in any way stain the sky, or like a face's expressions, peaceful or wrathful, reflected in a mirror that cannot in any way modify, for good or ill, the mirror itself. If one does not understand that this is so and takes things to be truly existent, the results of such a mistake are what we call "samsara," "ignorance," "the blank, indeterminate state," or the "universal ground." On the other hand, if one refrains from taking things as truly existent, then— even without the application of antidotes—they subside naturally and give way to "nirvana," "awareness," "primordial wisdom," and "dharmakāya." The wild and mighty yogi Drukpa Kunlek[79] has said,

> Primal purity, awareness—the ignorant, amorphous state—
> For Kunlek there is nothing else to meditate.

And in the tantra, we find it said that "the states of ignorance and primordial wisdom are not two different things."

Consequently, it is in one's own mind that one must distinguish samsara from nirvana. If one is able to do this, then whatever manifests—the outer phenomena of the six consciousnesses; the inner attitude of adopting or rejecting them; and the defilements, thoughts, and so on at the secret level—is the display of ultimate reality, the dharmatā. It is the expression of that same ultimate reality. Although it arises, it arises from unborn ultimate reality. Although it remains, it remains in unborn ultimate reality. Although it ceases, it ceases in unborn ultimate reality. One may therefore be deluded, but one is deluded in the state of ultimate reality. One may gain liberation, but one does so in the state of ultimate reality. If one were to search for even an atom of some kind of "phenomenon" different from ultimate reality, one would not find it. And in itself, the ultimate reality of things falls outside the scope of the ordinary mind; it transcends the conceived object endowed with characteristics that can be expressed and thought about. It is inconceivable and indestructible, like the very heart of space. It is as Tilopa said,

Kyého!
This is primal wisdom self-cognizing,
Beyond the range of speech, beyond the sphere of mind.
There's nothing I Tilopa have to show;
For you should know that it reveals itself.

Whatever good or bad thoughts appear within the state of ulti-mate reality—like waves arising and sinking back into the sea—they arise as the play of the dharmakāya and so [in themselves] they can bring neither benefit nor harm. As it is said in the *Songs of Realization*,[80] "The uncontrived mind is ever-present, and yogis should understand [such thoughts] like water poured into water." If one has such an understanding, this constitutes the most import-ant crucial point of all practices: using the six consciousnesses, hap-piness and suffering, sickness, the five poisons, thoughts, and so on as the path. Therefore, without examining the outer object [for one has concluded that the object's appearance is in the mind itself], one settles one's mind without adopting or rejecting anything, and without applying remedial antidotes. It is thus that all thoughts and appearances will arise as ultimate reality, the dharmatā.

As Lingje Repa[81] has said,

If you settle in a state that's fresh and uncontrived,
    realization will occur.
If you keep it like a flowing stream, it will manifest completely.
Relinquish characteristics, all conceptual targets.
Remain in even meditation, you who practice!

This refers to mindfulness, genuine and effortless. And as the lord and siddha Sherab Yarphel has said,

If there's no need, when thoughts arise,
To bring my mind back,
This, I understand, is mindfulness that's uncontrived.

There does not exist a more profound method for causing the phenomenal appearances of the postmeditational state to arise as primordial wisdom. As it is said in the *Six Aims of Meditation*,[82]

> Whatever thoughts occur, if one can understand
> That they are ultimate reality,
> There is no need to meditate on dharmakāya otherwise.

Some people of lesser mental capacity, however, fail to acquire a full experience of this and, clinging to their theoretical understanding and to the side of emptiness, they confine their minds within but leave appearances outside—greatly separating apprehended objects from the apprehending subject. They meditate on emptiness alone but are unable to meditate on appearing phenomena [as the locus of the union of appearance and emptiness]. They are agitated by the thoughts produced by the contriving mind, and they pass through many different experiences, high or low. When this occurs, such practitioners should not dwell on the emptiness aspect of the mind but instead should focus on the [emptiness of] external objects that appear and generate the defilements of craving and aversion together with the experience of happiness and suffering. By training in this way, they will progress. It is said too that this is a means whereby *freedom from conceptual construction* may be enhanced into the state of *one taste*.[83]

Again, there are some who because they do not recognize the nature of their mind and because they have no devotion for their teacher are bereft of inner experience. Instead, they place their trust in the mere understanding of books and being unsatisfied with simply preserving the nature of the mind or awareness in its natural flow, they claim that it is only when something bad (which they refer to as the "ordinary mind") is eliminated that something clear and limpid called "awareness," or *rigpa*, will be obtained. And they cling to the luminous and empty state of mind between two thoughts, with mouths gaping and eyes staring into space—their mental sight at the mercy of their wind energies. The end result is that they fail to accomplish the Great Perfection and succeed only in disturbing their life-wind. They do not know—they do not understand—anything.[84] If they meditate, their heart has no delight; if they give it up, they have no peace of mind. Nothing works, whatever they might try, and in the end, they go completely crazy. There are lots of people like this nowadays.

Therefore, one should not get bogged down in too many elaborate reflections about *śamatha* and *vipaśyanā*, the ordinary mind, and awareness. The mind should not be focused too strenuously. Instead, the main thing to remember is that if, with respect and devotion to one's teacher, one can simply leave the "plain and ordinary mind of the present moment" (*tha mal gyi shes pa*),[85] the state of fresh awareness, to itself in its natural flow, and if one is able to disregard, without any concern, whatever experiences occur, this itself is the most profound experience of all.

In short, whether it is the object that appears in the mind, or the mind that appears as the object, it all comes down to the same thing. If, relying on perfect, effortless mindfulness, one settles in whatever arises without rejecting or indulging in it, one will finally realize the inseparability of appearance and mind and the single taste of manifold things. And even that which is the agent of such a realization will become groundless and rootless. Ultimate reality, which is the object of meditation, and the mind that meditates on it will blend together in the single state of nonduality. And so it is that without meditation one will reign supreme in the kingdom of the dharmakāya.

Gotsangpa, lord of Dharma, teaches us the same crucial point.

> Essentially, whatever happiness or sorrow, whatever fault or quality, whatever help or harm may befall you, simply relax and settle in it, without rejection or indulgence. Things appear in the mind; they have no substantial existence apart from it. Keep to this way of practicing, mindfully and without distraction. Moreover, at the time of the four yogas,[86] you should act as

follows. When you are practicing *one-pointedness*, tenacious mindfulness is the most important thing. When you are in the *freedom from conceptual construction*, the point is to be mindful of emptiness. That is, when desire or aversion manifests, their emptiness is called to mind. In this practice of freedom from conceptual construction, things are necessarily seen as empty and emptiness is therefore considered to be of prime importance. There is, nevertheless, an aspect of effort in this regard. When you experience *single taste*, a perfect and effortless mindfulness arises with regard to discursive thought. Since the thoughts that arise are the meditation itself, no effort is involved. There is no need to remind yourself that thoughts *are* ultimate reality, the dharmatā. In the postmeditation period, phenomena are perceived as mere illusions. And when emptiness is seen to be the very principle of karmic cause and effect, and when karmic cause and effect arise as emptiness, you are close to a state of mindfulness beyond the ordinary mind. Finally, in the yoga of *no meditation*, mindfulness beyond the ordinary mind actually occurs, and at that point, whatever appears as an external object is not even taken as an illusion.

When you practice, you fully understand, thanks to the kindness of your teacher, that your own mind—namely, all the thoughts that arise—is groundless and rootless. And you remain in this understanding. If a thought arises, you rest in the recognition of its nature. Apart from continuously preserving this state, there is nothing else for you to do.

At that time, because your space-like mind, free of the dualistic cognitions of apprehender and apprehended, is not regarded as yourself, generosity is perfected. Since the mind is not stained by faults and downfalls, discipline is perfected. Since you are not afflicted by thoughts of happiness and suffering, patience is perfected. Since you remain in this state without distraction, diligence is perfected. Since there is no difference between meditation and postmeditation, meditative stability is perfected. And since this state is free from delusion, wisdom is perfected.

The six cycles of even taste are also perfected. Given that they arise as the dharmakāya, thoughts are taken as the path. Since the five poisons subside in primordial wisdom, defilement is taken as the path. Since it is understood that all the obstacles, the work of gods and spirits, are just one's own mind, these same gods and spirits are fearlessly taken as the path. Since whatever manifests arises as great bliss, all suffering is taken as the path. Since there is neither pain nor grief, illness is taken as the path. Since there is no difference between meditation and postmeditation, there is no thought either of birth or of death, which means that death itself is taken as the path.

In the same vein, Sherab Yarphel, the great siddha of Shechen, said,

> If you realize the mental state beyond elaboration,
> This is the Madhyamaka.
> If you realize the single taste of all phenomena,
> This is Mahāmudrā.
> If you realize the fundamental state that's free from
>   meditation,
> This is Mahāsaṅdhi.[87]
> How freedom happens in these three great states I now
>   explain.
> If you are freed through mindfulness,
> This is Mahāsaṅdhi.
> If the view is linked with clinging, it is not the view.
> If you are freed through mental stillness,

This is Mahāmudrā.
If meditation's linked with forceful mindfulness, it is not
    the meditation.
If you are freed through mental movement,
This is the Madhyamaka.
If action's linked with clinging,[88] it is not the action.

And he also said,

Let me speak straightforwardly. This is how it is.
For those endowed with wisdom, there's no view.
For those who reach the *bhumis'* end, there is no
    meditation.
For those who are beyond these two, there is no action.
And how, without these three, could there be a result?

If, in fact, these four are present, it is not the ultimate.
They are, so it is said, the pleasure ground of childish beings.
View, meditation, action—to wish and hope for these
Is an exhausting illness, so the teachings say.
Relax at ease, you'll find vast space within—how
    wonderful!

For the view without a center and circumference,
Supreme is meditation that is free of reference.
For action that is targetless,
Nonattainment is the supreme fruit.
To have no view—this is the supreme view.
To have no meditation is the supreme meditation.
To have no action is the supreme action.
These three "supremes" inseparable are said to be the highest
    fruit.

To list to no extreme—this is the highest view.
Luminosity without conception is the highest meditation.

The collapse of all intended action is the highest action.
Purity and luminosity united are said to be the highest fruit.

For the view that's free from clinging,
To have no target is the best of meditations.
For action that is free from all intended acts,
To have no gain or loss, this is the supreme fruit.

For the view that's rootless, empty from the outset,
The self-subsiding of conceptual features is the supreme
    meditation.
For action free from expectation,
Truly not to act with an intention is the highest fruit.[89]

No-self is the supreme view.
To have no notions and no object is the supreme meditation.
To have no agent is the supreme action.
Nothing purged and nothing gained—this is the supreme
    fruit.

For mindfulness of ultimate reality, primordially empty,
The collapse of ordinary perceptions is supreme.
If you can meditate unmoving on the fundamental nature,
You will achieve enlightenment, there is no doubt.

To want the view, to want the meditation,
To want the action—when these three occur,
It's said to be delusion.
If I now explain, it is like this:

It is not wrong to have quite naturally
The view that sees the fundamental state.
For, by itself, it's just the mind's own nature.
But when the *wish* to have the view occurs,
This is an adventitious ego-clinging thought.

And likewise, it's not wrong to rest within
The natural flow of meditation;
It's just the natural condition of the mind itself.
But when the *wish* to meditate occurs,
This is an adventitious thought that clings to meditation.

And there's no harm in freely practicing[90]
The view and meditation.
It's just the nondual situation of the mind itself.
But when the *wish* to practice comes,
It's just the adventitious spreading out of dualistic
    thought—
Delusions and deluded clinging without interruption.

If briefly said, the view, the meditation, and the action,
All three are good when they occur quite naturally.
And yet to want the view, the meditation, and the action
Is understood to be defective.
For it is mental action centered on the self,
Whereas primordial wisdom is beyond the mind.

In the instant you are mindful of the nature of the mind,
There is no apprehender-apprehended.
Meditation, action—both are easy.
But in the second instant when this clarity of mind
Is agitated, it is hard for emptiness and bliss to happen.

As long as there is subject-object dualistic clinging,
Phenomena are recognized as this or that,
Discursive thought is not transcended.
And through torpor, dullness, drowsiness,
Mindfulness is vague and hazy.
And even though you train yourself,
In such a situation, you will not gain freedom.

As long as there is hope to see or fear to miss
The fundamental way of things,
How can you see the true state
Of appearances and emptiness united?

As long as *ālaya*, the universal ground, is present,
You will fail to see the utterly pure nature.
But when the view of one's own level, vajra-like,
Has overwhelmed the ālaya,
Awareness and the vast expanse will not be seen as two.

If this is your aspiration, you should act as follows.
With nondual all-perceiving wisdom,
You should repeatedly destroy the mind
That apprehends conceptual attributes of things.
And when the view is realized,
If your mind is left unaltered, simultaneous will be
The arising and dissolving of your thoughts.
In the instant they appear, they will directly cease.
However short may be the meditation, progress will be great.

All that should be known
As the important points for practice
May now be briefly stated.
If the limpid wisdom of the yogi
Is unable to distinguish attributes of things,
Then though appearances of subject-object cease,
It's just the state of Hoshang,[91]
Destitute of all-perceiving wisdom.

Those who have completed all the grounds of realization,
May well be free of thoughts and all mentation,
But they are not without the all-perceiving wisdom.
Their outer conduct is suffused with discipline,

They strive in learning and reflection.
Their inner conduct is to practice in retreat
The generation and perfection stages.
Their secret conduct is to practice Great Perfection,
Wherein the practices of trekchö and of thögal
Are most secret and supreme.
Than this there is no better teaching.

To experience *one-pointedness*[92] is a constraining sheath.
Though you may meditate and meditate on empty
    luminosity,
Whether faults or qualities will come is quite uncertain.
It is best to follow an authentic teacher.

When you leave behind the sheath of the experience
Of the *freedom from conceptual construction*,
Although this is the time when there's no misconception
Of phenomena, unborn and empty,
It should be understood
That mingling appearances with emptiness is best.

In the *single taste*, the mind blends with appearance.
Since good and bad are not distinguished,
Nothing need be purged or added.
Meditation, action—both are easy.
And yet the clear distinction of phenomena is best.

No meditation is the time when stains are purified.
Though view and meditation are both free of effort,
Awareness self-cognizing, pure and luminous,
Takes firmly hold of freedom from conceptual construction.
This—it should be understood—is best.

Much has been explained about the mind,
And yet, without associating past and future thoughts,

When you directly and immediately recognize
The wisdom [that results from meditation],
This itself is self-arisen primal wisdom.
Inwardly relaxing without hope or fear,
You should simply stay in free and natural rest.

Indeed, not leaving what appears outside,
And not confining your own mind within,
Thoughts about appearances subside.
When there is no first appearance and no later emptiness,
This state is called the "union of the two truths."
The utterly pure nature of the mind is found therein.

"Very well, [some say], the mind meets with appearance
But does not mix with it."
But if the meditating mind is kept within
And the appearance on which it meditates is left elsewhere,
Examining and searching thoughts will come
And calm abiding will be lost.
Mindfulness will struggle with distraction
And there will be no penetrating insight.
Not sundering appearances and mind,
You should practice "stillness, movement, mindfulness."

Sherab Yarphel also said,

Éma!
If now I sing to you a song of my experience and realization,
Definitive and certain freedom is like this.
When awareness self-cognizing
Is kindled in the ultimate expanse,
Outwardly the dharmakāya shines
And inwardly there is the universal ground.
Seeing these two things, I am amazed!
As I rest relaxed within a natural state of mind,

I sometimes see the limpid, brilliant luminosity
Of the consciousness of the universal ground.
I do not understand this as the final view;
I simply keep the radiance
Of "plain and ordinary mind."[93]
At moments of great drowsiness and sinking,
I am enveloped in the universal ground,
And mindfulness diminishes;
View, meditation, action—all lack clarity.
It's then that, as my path, I take the luminosity
Of awareness's own radiance.
Sometimes when the nature of the mind
Appears spontaneously,
Or else when I can use it as the path,
The universal ground subsides into the dharmakāya,
And there I understand the final view.
And even though at times there are distractions,
Like waves that swell upon the sea,
These same distractions do not fall
Outside of ultimate reality.
So it is that I have understood a crucial point
Of seeing the mind's nature.

In short, at all times I now see
That various and uncertain views and meditations
Are just like grasping at the sky with one's own hands.
But when I do not strive in all such meditations,
It's then I see the actual nature in itself,
The changeless fundamental mode of things.
When the raiment of the attributes
Of dual appearance is removed,
Awareness self-cognizing is seen nakedly to soar.
When I am able to remain quite freely in the natural state,
I see the objects of six consciousnesses
Arising naturally, as they are.

When, once thoughts arise,
I do not have to bring my mind back,
This, I understand, is keeping to the nature uncontrived.
If I am without hope or fear, and if I do not alter anything,
I realize that this is to see
This nature nakedly without fixation.
If recognizing it, I can relax in it,
I understand this as primordial purity.

If, my child, you are too tense,
You will be hindered in postmeditation;
The time will never come
For seeing the two truths in union.
But if you are too loose,
Your meditation will decline;
Your mind will certainly be blank and dull.
Therefore, neither tense nor loose,
Preserve your "plain and ordinary mind," my child.

Do not reflect and do not meditate,
But simply rest within your true condition.
It's important to be carefree and relaxed.
With undistracted mindfulness,
Be watchful from afar.
This is the final and true path, my child.
If you are skilled in growing used to this,
You will undoubtedly obtain
A true cessation, dharmakāya.

When you preserve the uncontrived,
Fresh state of mindfulness,
It's then that you will recognize
Primordial wisdom self-arisen.
If earlier thoughts do not give rise to later ones,
However many may arise,

They will be virtuous qualities.

Sherab Yarphel also said,

> Those who spend their whole lives
> Practicing the sacred Dharma
> Will not regret it even if
> They have to go to the three lower realms.
>
> Those who for the sake of Dharma
> Offer all that they possess
> Will not regret it even if
> They die of cold and hunger.
>
> Those who have the Dharma in their minds
> And do not cling to all the many pleasures of this life
> Will not regret it even if
> They have to suffer in the bardo.
>
> Those whose acts are pleasing
> To authentic masters
> Will not regret it even if
> Their final years are marked by madness and dementia.
>
> Those who do no evil
> For their own or general purposes
> Will not regret it even if
> The people call them ineffective and pathetic.
>
> Those who do not cling
> To this life's friends or foes
> Will not regret it even if
> Desire and anger manifest upon the moment of their
>   death.

Those who think that pleasure, pain, prosperity, decline
Are all the consequence of actions in the past
Will not regret it even if
Their later fortunes turn to ill.

If your mind and Dharma mingle,
Virtuous will be your every deed,
And you will not regret it even if
You do not do much "virtuous practice."

If on the Triple Gem
You constantly rely,
You will not regret it even if
The Lord of Death springs on you unannounced.

If you have but little clinging
To your friends, companions, and possessions,
You will not regret it even if
The public thinks you ignorant and blundering.

If you are skilled in taming your own mind—
Its desire for pleasure and its fear of pain—
You won't regret the fact that you're not good
At sticking with your cronies, beating up your enemies.

If you are bereft of craving and of grasping,
Guarding what you have and seeking what you lack,
You won't regret it even when they say
You've no idea how to make and keep your wealth.

If you can never have enough of Dharma
And are skilled in shunning sin,
You'll be without regret regarding
Your good actions and the wisdom of your ways.

If, through acting thus,
Your thoughts are untouched by regret,
The joy you take in virtuous deeds
Will prosper and increase.

If, when you practice virtue, illness strikes
Or else some mental anguish hard to bear,
You will find comfort in the thought
That these are signs that evil karma is exhausted.

If, the teachings say, you did not have such karmic residues,
You would have no mindfulness of Dharma.
Conversely, if you have it,
Various obstacles, provoked by Mara, enter in.

People, though they're weak, perhaps one hundred years old,
Think only of their needs for this, their present life.
Rare are those who think of death
And practice virtue for a little while.

Specifically, because of karma,
There is nothing certain.
Some, when young, have few attachments and desires.
But as they age, their wants and cravings grow.

Some, as evil karma bursts forth in their lives,
Neglect the thought of death
And for the sake of this, their present life,
Accomplish every kind of wicked deed.

Some are without sorrow for samsara
And have no wish to leave it.
Swollen with false views,
They are completely destitute of faith.

Some there are who, constantly
Beneath the power of demons,
Are unable to distinguish good from ill,
They are greatly troubled by five poisons.

Arrogant, self-satisfied,
They mix with irreligious folk.
They indulge in speculation
On the inconceivable and inexpressible.

Though they enter monasteries
And institutes of learning,
When at first they hear profound instruction,
They feel bored and tired.

Later, they may study, and acquire some understanding,
But they are impervious, deriving no great benefit.
They keep company with male and female householders,
Competing with them in their worldly ways.

Even for an instant it is hard for them
To keep their thoughts and deeds in harmony with
    Dharma.
In short, all men and women, high and low,
Fear only loss and poverty in this, their present life.
It's hard for them to have a single thought
Of benefiting others in their future lives.

And even if, by karmic accident,
The thought of Dharma comes to them,
They postpone their practice till a later date
And thus deceive themselves.

Sherab Yarphel also said,

Kayé!
When one has, for one's own sake, accomplished
    dharmakāya,
It is said that, for the sake of others,
One must have unbounded skill in means,
As well as the four ways whereby disciples are assembled.
But I, before I've tamed my own mind,
Think that I can tame the minds of others!

But when I point the finger inwardly
And my own mind investigate, I find there many faults.
My realization brings no freedom.
My realization's just an empty boast.
It's really strange—a toad that claims to be a lion!
The proud, the teachings say, are quite unable
To progress into the vast expanse, the view of evenness.
"Just rest yourself at ease," I tell myself,
Till inner signs have manifested outwardly.
Still many marvelous things are there to see,
How wonderful!

In the same vein, Tenphel,[94] also a great siddha of Shechen, also
said,

When outwardly you see how wealth and pleasures change,
And inwardly you are without a need for anything,
Of every kind of generosity, this is the king.
Now you need not gather funds for acts of generosity.

When outwardly you see how fleeting are phenomena,
And inwardly you're able to cut through your craving and
    attachment,
This has been proclaimed the king of every practice.
Now you have no need of strenuous meditation.

If outwardly, through deep and skillful methods,
You're able to assimilate the crucial points,
And inwardly you know how you should act
In the awareness state,
This is the profound practice of the Secret Mantra.
Now even taking meat and alcohol, you're fine.

If outwardly you understand that in samsara and nirvana,
All lacks true existence,
And inwardly you know that there is nothing to be
    meditated,
This is the final understanding of the sutras and the
    tantras.
Now even without all the great texts, you are fine.

If outwardly you understand that all the beings
Of the six realms are your fathers and your mothers,
And inwardly you're able to exert yourself
In ways that bring them benefit,
This is the mental training of the bodhisattvas.
Now you have no use for speeches on compassion.

If outwardly you know that what appears is an illusion,
And inwardly you're able to maintain the unborn
    fundamental nature,
This is indeed awareness, the teacher true and ultimate.
Now you do not need to look for other teachers.

If outwardly you understand
That all that can be talked about is like an echo,
And inwardly you understand
The sense of what cannot be talked about,
This is the greatest of all understandings.
Now even if you do not study, all is well.

If outwardly you see your body
As an empty mountain hermitage,
And inwardly your mind does not get lost
In circumstantial happenings,
This is the supreme and perfect solitude.
Now you do not need to seek an outer hermitage.

If outwardly you do not cling to complex virtuous practices,
And inwardly you are without deluded hope and fear,
This is virtuous practice, ultimate and nonconceptual.
Now there's no need for a list of good deeds to be done!

If outwardly you give up clinging
To appearances, to sounds, and thoughts,
And inwardly you strive in emptiness, the dharmakāya,
This is the king of meditations.
Now you do not need to do retreat beset with many
    hardships.

If outwardly appearances are for you
A vast and boundless palace,
And inwardly you meditate that beings are all buddhas,
This is the instruction for the generation and perfection
    stages.
Now you need not meditate upon some other buddha
    field.

If outwardly you see appearances
As the trikāya buddha field,
And inwardly you stay immersed
Within the nature of the mind,
This is the true authentic triple-kāya buddha field.
Now you need not meditate upon some separate dharmakāya.

The siddha Tenphel also said,

I, a beggar, destitute, defenseless,
Pray constantly, without forgetting,
To the Triple Gem, my guardians undeceiving.
Thus I'm happy and dedicate my joy to wandering beings.
Relinquishing attachment to my happiness and pleasure,
I rest within the state that's free from pain and pleasure.
And even if some grief occurs,
I see it as the residue of former action,
And wish that it will cleanse away
The pains of all my mothers in the six migrations.
I, this crazy beggar, know what virtue is.
Now everything I do turns into virtuous practice.

And also,

You, my faithful followers, remember and rely
Upon this happy song of joy
Of me, a beggar-man.
I watch the mind, but nothing do I see.
Now even when I do not watch it,
There it is, quite clear.
I sleep now in a state
That cannot be described.
This is the view
Of me, a beggar-man.

To the luminosity of mind I do not cling.
Whatever this, my mind, may think,
Within the state of mind remains.
For mind that stirs not from itself
There's naught on which to meditate.
No meditation then is this my meditation.

Unvirtuous action I have laid aside.
All deeds to virtue have I turned.

Nonaction, then—it's there I rest at ease.
This is the action of myself,
An old man, fond and foolish.

With mind devoted, free of guile,
With true joy and a yearning for the teachings,
I plant the flag of victory:
The practice of a single life—
This is the samaya pledge of me, a yogi.

In the field of the Victorious One,
I purify my mothers, beings of the six migrations.
My body, speech, and mind arise
As deity, mantra, dharmakāya.
I sleep now in a state devoid of hope and fear.
Such is the fruit that I, the realized yogi, gained.

If, once again, I scrutinize their meaning,
View, meditation, action, and result,
Are all now nowhere else than in my mind.
And in the dharmakāya, unborn nature of my mind,
Awareness self-cognizing is Samantabhadra,
Who appears and works the benefit
Of wandering beings without understanding.
What a laugh! The action and the agent—
Are they something other than myself?
I sleep now in the state that's free of clinging.
And with a mind free to its utter depth,
I plant the victory flag of my accomplishment.

Whatever deed you do, act only virtuously
And rest at ease; who cares what others say?
These words come from my heart,
My dear, beloved, friends.
Were I to offer you my own red heart,

What difference would there be?
It is the heart blood of a thousand mother ḍākinīs.
Put it into practice, that is my request.

As a brief summary, Dharmaradza,[95] the great Dharma lord of
Shechen, said,

In the main practice, leave your natural mind
Unmixed with states contrived by intellect,
Preserving thus the "plain and ordinary mind"
That's free from something watched and one who
    watches.
Aside from this there's not one atom to be meditated.
Whatever thoughts may manifest
They sink back in the very moment of arising,
Just like waves subsiding in the water.
If caught by your awareness, thoughts
Are like designs traced on the flood.
If watched and watcher both are found
To be devoid of ground and root,
It is the sign that you have practiced.
And here the most important point
Is to preserve this state but have no grasping—
No thought that it is something good.
If you train like this repeatedly,
Even without meditation,
You can never lose the radiance of awareness.
Then without meditation, without mental wandering,
The realization of the ultimate reality
Beyond the ordinary mind will come to you.
If the grime of thoughts has not been cleaned away,
There is no realization of awareness, primal wisdom.
To know how to distinguish
Awareness from the ordinary mind—
This is a special feature of the Great Perfection teachings.

Since there's nothing to be seen through watching,
Just rest in the condition of the watcher.
Don't "meditate" but keep the radiance of awareness.
Give up all two-faced conduct,
Abandon all accepting and rejecting.
You do not have to strain for the result,
For there it is complete within you.
With unwavering devotion, supplicate
Your teacher, take the four empowerments.
Mix your mind with his and rest in meditation.
The mind-transcending dharmakāya
Will arise within you.
This counsel from my heart
Distills the key points of the practice.

He also said,

When you dwell in solitude,
My child, do not act carelessly.
Be deeply disenchanted with samsara,
And rely completely on the Triple Gem.
Give rise to love, compassion, bodhichitta—train in them.
And from your heart invoke your teacher, your true father.
Not letting your mind wander where it will,
Hold it with the ropes of mindfulness and vigilance.
If, not staying in retreat, you wander through the villages,
And go into retreat just for the sake of looking good,
Such posturing will waste your human life.
Don't let yourself do much of that!

The mind is the root of all phenomena.
Looking for its nature, you will see that it is empty.
Its movements all subside
Within the state of emptiness and luminosity.
But do not impose stillness, do not halt its movement.

No matter what arises,
Rest free of alteration or contrivance.
No matter what appearances arise,
Objects of six consciousnesses,
Just leave them where they are,
Neither block nor welcome them.
If you do not fix on them,
They will be just like magical illusions.
What confusion to construct a dam for mirage water!
When obstacles occur and situations good or bad,
Pray to your teacher, your dear father, constantly.
When you need to dissipate some hindrance
And enhance your practice,
Search in the texts, the discourses of teachers, lords of
    Dharma.
When sadness and dejection fall on you in solitude,
Read about the lives of previous siddhas.
Now in this moment, when you're free and independent,
Make sure that sacred Dharma comes to birth in you.
By the time that sickness comes, and death,
You must have gained undaunted confidence.
If in this brief time of your human life,
You don't achieve the ultimate objective,
But let yourself be borne away by worldly things,
Than this there is no greater failure.
Now that you have met the Buddha
In the person of your teacher,
If you do not have devotion and one-pointed faith,
But criticize and entertain wrong views,
Than this there is no greater evil.
Now that for once you have both freedoms and advantages,
If you spend your life in negativity and fail to practice
    virtue,
There is no way of living that is worse than this.
If in this brief and passing life,

You spend your days with eyes and tongue distracted,
And squander all your nights away in sleep,
There's no mistake as great as this.
Now's the time to strive for your own sake.
If you don't prepare yourself
So that, at death, you will have no regret,
Your human life is squandered—
There's no greater loss than this.
For everyone within the three samsaric worlds,
At the end of each and every life,
There's nowhere else to go but death—
And at that time there is no help but Dharma.
Compounded things are hollow, essenceless,
And endless are samsaric deeds.
However much you have, you're never satisfied.
There is no end to what the mind desires.
And though you hoard all your possessions,
You cannot take them with you when you die.
There is no way to bear the sorrows of the lower destinies.
Other than your teacher, there's no other hope.
And so be constant and courageous.
Make sure to gain your everlasting bliss.

These are the words of Dharmaradza. Moreover, as the Master from Orgyen, knower of the three times, has said, it is important not to lose one's view in action or one's action in the view. And so, while in meditation, one should confidently settle in the state of meditative evenness. Then, in the postmeditation periods, one's behavior should correspond to what has been said in all the various sections of the teaching, according to one's level of experience. Chiefly, one should lay the foundation with ethical discipline and come to a clear conviction by means of the view. One should practice with concentration and enhance one's experience with devotion and respect. The hindrances that arise from hopes and fears and the belief in the true existence of things should be eliminated, and as an ancillary to this, one should adopt as one's path a behavior based on the "equal taste" of all things. The constant determination to escape from samsara and the remembrance of impermanence and death should be one's incitement to practice. One should never at any time lose the states of mindfulness, vigilance, and carefulness. One should train without error on the entire path in which emptiness and compassion, wisdom and skillful means, and the generation and perfection stages are united inseparably. One should make use of whatever may act as an antidote to ego-clinging and defilement, and defilements should be eliminated, transformed, or used as the path, according to one's capacity of mind. One should always equalize the eight worldly concerns and keep to the lowest place. One should refrain from criticizing either the teachings or people. One should reverence everyone—good, bad, and mediocre—on the crown of one's head. Whatever happens, happiness, sorrow, illness, and so on should be understood as the result of past actions and should be pressed into service on the path. Whatever may befall, one should not allow the Dharma to fall beneath its sway. Finally, with the excellent attitude of bodhichitta for the sake of beings, one should, on a vast scale, make prayers of aspiration for the good of others.

If inwardly one subdues defilement and furthers the practice as much as possible without others even noticing it, this itself subsumes all the crucial points of the practice.

All this idle talk of qualities I do not have—
How can it be of any good to others?
If those with knowledge see it, I shall be ashamed—
And you are someone who has studied,
You're endowed with Dharma eyes!
Yet you're the one who asked for it.
You're the one who banged the drum!
So this I now present to you.
Please take it, my pure offering of faith,
And when you see its faults, forgive me.

I make a prayer that, by this virtue,
We may come to the primordial realm.

At the request of Jigme Drayang, my great spiritual friend, who
is rich in the qualities that flow from the three trainings, I, Pema
Namgyal, an old monk of Shechen, composed this text drawing on
some passages taken from the teachings of past learned and accomplished masters of the same monastery. Virtue!

3

A Pith Instruction on the
Great Perfection for Beginners

I bow in homage to the Second Buddha, the omniscient Lord of Speech, Longchen Rabjam of the glorious foundation of Samyé.

It is now time to give a brief explanation of the crucial points of the actual practice of the Great Perfection. To begin with, the crucial point related to the body is that you should sit on a comfortable seat, relaxed and at ease, in the seven-point posture of Vairocana. In particular, since the eyes are the gateway for the arising of primordial wisdom, you should not use any visual support but gaze directly ahead into space. The crucial point of speech is that you should allow yourself to breathe quite naturally, not through the nose but very gently through the mouth. There are important reasons of each of these key points, and it is imperative that you do not treat them lightly.

As a preliminary step, cultivate feelings of sadness and weariness with samsara, decide that you will turn away from it forever, and develop feelings of compassion and the attitude of bodhichitta.

Then meditate on your teacher in his or her ordinary form, seated on a lotus and a disk of the moon above the crown of your head. Pray to your teacher that the extraordinary realization of the profound path take birth swiftly in your mind—with such devotion that you have tears in your eyes. Mere words and lip service are of no use. For the realization of the Great Perfection to arise in you, it is essential to receive blessings from a teacher belonging to that lineage. And since the reception of blessings depends on the devotion of the disciple, this alone is the most important factor. So without any complacency with regard to all the recitations and practices you may have been able to complete, you should pray to your teacher with great fervor. Finally, while adopting the appropriate visualizations, you should receive the four empowerments from him or her and, mingling inseparably your mind with his or hers, you should maintain, free of all fixation, the state of the great bliss of the fundamental nature, empty but luminous.

This does not mean that you are meditating in the blank and indeterminate state of the universal ground. Neither are you meditating in the state of the consciousness of the universal ground, which is simply clear and aware. Nor are you training in a dazed experience of no-thought. It also does not mean that you are meditating in a state in which thoughts about all kinds of things, occurring as mental objects, are in constant movement.

So what is this meditation like? When the previous thought has ended, the later one has not arisen, and you are unconcerned with the one occurring in the present, there comes a bare, self-cognizing awareness, a spacious state in which luminosity and emptiness are united. This is the mind-transcending primordial purity of the trekchö path of the Great Perfection. It is a naked state of openness in which the phenomena [of samsara and nirvana] are exhausted.

When this state has been recognized, the practice consists in relaxing and settling in its natural flow. You need to know how to lay it bare nakedly in any situation, whether of view, meditation, or action. Some who are unable to do this might say that it is a state without arising, dwelling, and ceasing. Others, thinking it is this or that, contrive a name for what is in fact nameless. They are ensnared in the traps of mental activity, and the moment of realization will never come to them. Words and reasoning can establish only what is no more than an idea of the naked dharmakāya, mind-transcending, empty, and aware. When, however, the blessings of a teacher meet with the strength of your meditation, you will be able, after some time, to cut through your inner misconceptions just like a child reaching the point where it can think clearly for itself. This is why it is so important to persevere continuously in your meditation without ever abandoning it.

If, as a beginner in the practice, you are too relaxed, there is a danger of falling into an ordinary profusion of thoughts. You should therefore rely on mindfulness, never forgetting to be vigilant. Whether your mind is still, moving, or mindful [of these two states], it is important to meditate, watching nakedly that which recognizes these states, in other words, your fresh awareness. When you meditate in this way, the sign that your awareness is relaxed will be that you will feel that you have more wild and agitated thoughts and defilements than before and endless experiences of bliss, clarity, and no-thought will occur. But if, in a state that is free from expectation and apprehension, you can refrain from fixating on these experiences, accepting some and rejecting others, and if, as you meditate, you watch nakedly the awareness whence these experiences arise, these same experiences will become the friends [of your meditation]. If, on the other hand, you become fixated, you will be bound and fettered.

If your mind becomes too drowsy and dull and loses all clarity of awareness, you should meditate on the syllable *A* or a ball of light in your heart. Imagine that this shoots up through the crown of your head and hovers in the space about an arrow's length above your head. Keeping this in mind, hold your breath outside. This is the way to get rid of drowsiness and dullness. If, on the other hand, your mind is too agitated, you should relax deep inside your body and mind. Lower your gaze and visualize a point of light at the tip of your nose. This will get rid of agitation.

Sometimes, moreover, when the sky is cloudless and limpidly clear, you should turn your back to the sun and focus your eyes on the middle of the sky. Breathe very slowly and hold your breath outside. And in an instant, the naked dharmakāya, empty, aware, and unimpeded, will manifest from within you. This extremely profound pith instruction is called the "wisdom of the threefold space" (*nam kha' sum phrugs kyi dgongs pa*).[96]

Alternatively, you could adopt the seven-point posture and, breathing naturally, rest your mind for an instant in a nonconceptual state. Then, stretching out your arms and legs, lie on your back and look into space. Pronounce the syllable *Ha* strongly three times, expel your breath, and let your mind settle in its natural condition. A nonconceptual wisdom will arise in which all phenomena are exhausted.

Or again, settling [your mind] naturally as before and sitting in the seven-point posture, if you refrain from resting with the appearance of whatever occurs and if, with your gaze lowered, you settle relaxed and free in the emptiness of that appearance—in other words, if you settle in a state of wide-open clarity in which there is no division between outside and inside—a realization of emptiness similar to space will manifest.

Or again, if, without settling your mind on the emptiness aspect, you place it without any clinging on the clear appearance [of what you are cognizing], you will come to the realization that the appearance is ungraspable and insubstantial.

Or again, if you focus on the movement of thoughts arising within your limpid awareness, these same thoughts, like waves sinking back into the water, will subside all by themselves in a state that is free of support and fixation. It is thus that you will gain realization. These experiences arise strongly and suddenly and are consequently profound skillful means for producing a confident certainty within yourself.

In brief, the indwelling samadhi of awareness mentioned above—the state of primordial purity in which phenomena are exhausted—is a state that transcends both virtue and nonvirtue, good qualities and bad, a state that is beyond both confirmation and refutation, and movement and change. This state is primordial wisdom. It transcends the mind caught in dualistic cognition. It is the ultimate goal of realization of Madhyamaka, Mahāmudrā, and Mahāsandhi. This awareness is something that we possess at all times. To recognize it and to preserve it without becoming tightly concentrated through deliberate effort, and without becoming too agitated through distraction—in other words, to maintain this recognition in an uncontrived and natural flow as a continuous stream-like yoga—is the very essence of the practice.

In that situation, whatever arises, the cognitions linked with the six consciousnesses, the five poisons, the increase or decrease of meditative experience, and so on—all such things manifest as the display of the creative power of awareness, the enlightened mind. They are like rainbows in the sky or waves upon the water. As appearances, they are all equal in that they appear. As empty, they are all equal in being empty. As true [on the relative level], they are all equal in being true, and as false illusions, they are all equal in being false. All things are none other than the manifestation of awareness. Therefore, you should neither indulge in them nor reject them; you should neither adopt nor discard them; you should not cling to antidotes in order to dispel them. When you relax in a fresh state of awareness from which all such things arise, everything that manifests will naturally subside. It is important to become proficient in this realization.

At that point, although the aspect of stillness is called "mental calm" (śamatha), and the aspect of realization of the naked, all-penetrating and empty awareness is called "deep insight" (vipaśyanā), the truth is that these twin aspects cannot be parted from each other. They are inseparable. When you understand that the nature of awareness is empty, you are released from the extreme of permanent existence. When you see the luminous character of awareness, you are released from the extreme of nonexistence, or nothingness. Since you do not pin your hopes on the meditative experiences of bliss, luminosity, and no-thought, you are freed from the three worlds.[97] And since all clinging to antidotes naturally dissipates, no deviations occur and there is nothing to veil the fundamental nature. You have no expectation of buddhahood at some later time, for this is something that happens only when you are trapped in the snare of reasoning and speculation. Instead, you use as the path the fact that, at this very moment, the three kāyas constitute your own natural birthright. This is a special instruction of the Great Perfection. For practitioners who have such an understanding, the sun of happiness arises from within, regardless of the circumstances in which they find themselves.

Now since all obstacles and deviations occur through hopes and fears, all of which derive from your grasping at the true existence of things, it is important not to cling to anything. Whatever happens, be it physical illness, mental sorrow, the obsessive fixation on defilement as though it were real, and all the ordinary attitudes of adopting and rejecting—you should first identify them and then pray to your teacher to grant his or her blessings. Then you should examine the experience, not roughly, but in detail, searching from where the mental state of accepting and rejecting arises, where it is occurring, and where it goes to when it disappears. If you search in this way, the naked dharmakāya, empty and aware, cannot fail to arise from within—the primordial wisdom that transcends the dualistic cognitions of subject and object, that does not exist as an entity, that does not dwell anywhere, and that cannot be expressed in words. When this happens, and while you are maintaining the presence of this state, all obstacles and deviations will subside all on their own.

The summit of all the practices, the purpose of which is to enhance your meditation, consists in devotion and respect for the teacher. It is therefore important not to consider your teacher as an ordinary person but to have a constant faith and a devotion that allows you to perceive him or her as a genuine buddha. In addition, if you meditate alternately on impermanence, compassion, the stages of generation and perfection, both conceptual and nonconceptual [that is, with characteristics and without characteristics],[98] these same meditations will enhance each other and be very effective. At the end of each session, you should dedicate your merit, and in the postmeditation period, you should at all times bring phenomena onto the path by considering them as magical illusions.

Regarding the sleep yoga practiced during the night, when you lie down, you should pray to experience your sleep as the state of luminosity, and you should mingle your mind with the mind of your teacher. And maintaining a state of fresh awareness uninterrupted by thoughts, you should [allow yourself to] fall asleep.

It is, moreover, crucial to understand that without the clear certainty of the view, your apprehension of, and clinging to, the true existence of apprehended objects and of the apprehending mind will not subside. When you are meditating, therefore, it is vital to settle with clear confidence in [the four vajra principles of] the nonexistence, the all-embracing evenness, the spontaneous presence, and the single nature of all phenomena (*med pa, phyal ba, lhun grub, gcig pu*).[99] Unless meditation is continually maintained, the mere fact of possessing awareness will not be sufficient to bring about the subsiding of dualistic experience. It is imperative to have constant diligence. And if in your behavior you do not make a clear distinction [between what is wholesome and what is not], there is a great danger that the only thing you will achieve will be to blather inanely about the emptiness of both virtue and nonvirtue. In the postmeditation periods, the crucial point is to consider that everything is dreamlike, while maintaining a steadfast certainty in the ineluctability of the karmic law of cause and effect. For it is thus that whatever you accomplish will be wholesome.

For as long as there is a division between skillful means and wisdom, you will be fettered [in samsara]. It is, therefore, important to set out on this excellent path, pleasing to the victorious ones, wherein emptiness and compassion and the accumulations of merit and wisdom are united.

These are all crucial points of the greatest importance. I therefore request you to keep them in your hearts.

If sadness with samsara and the thought of your impermanence
Do not arise within your mind,
And you remain engrossed in the deceptions of this life,
You will never realize true authentic Dharma.
May an uncontrived resolve to leave samsara
Take birth within your mind.

If you have no compassion,
If you are without the supreme bodhichitta,
You will live within the gloom of egocentric goals.
The Mahāyāna's perfect path will never manifest.
May you generate the supreme, pure enlightened mind.

If you do not reach the noble ground of realization,
You will only seem to be of benefit to others.
Not helping them, you will yourself be fettered.
Do not deceive yourself with busyness, distraction.
Instead with effort practice in a solitary place.

If skillful means and wisdom separate,
You will be like a person with broken legs.
You'll have no strength to journey to the level of omniscience.
Embark instead upon the path that unites without error
Emptiness, compassion; generation and perfection;
And the two accumulations.

Without the blessings of a master of a true, authentic lineage,
Even constant meditation will fail to bring forth realization
Of the fundamental nature.
Through connections marked with excellent devotion,
May you receive supreme empowerment
Of the mind to mind transmission.

Awareness self-cognizing, luminosity,
The Great Perfection that transcends the ordinary mind,
Is the presence, primordial, spontaneous,
Of the kāyas and the wisdoms.
Through the pith instruction
Of the four states uncontrived of "letting be,"
May you attain the everlasting kingdom
Of the state in which phenomena are all exhausted.

And when you gain this state wherein
You'll be of benefit to beings,
Don the armor of untiring patience in your work for others,
Thinking "From the river of existence, may I myself alone
Deliver all my mothers, limitless as space is vast."

This advice is given by a relaxed and happy yogi to his friend by the name of Kamala. It is intended as a pith instruction that might be of assistance to beginners.

Now it is complete. *Ithi.*

4

ANSWERS TO THE QUESTIONS OF
KHENPO JIGME DRAYANG

Namo Mañjuśrīye!

At the time of the primordial ground, which is common to both samsara and nirvana, the nature (*ngo bo*), the character (*rang bzhin*), and the cognitive potency (*thugs rje*) are all inseparable. This inseparability is the dharmatā, ultimate reality [in other words, awareness], which in turn is the great state of equality. That this is so is not necessarily realized. For it is like a man who by nature may possess a handsome form but who, until he encounters certain conditions, such as the presence of a mirror, will never be completely certain of how he looks. Since at the time of the common ground, there has as yet been no discarding of the ignorance that has the same nature [as awareness] and is the cause [of the other two kinds of ignorance][100]—for this ignorance is not itself present in the ground—and since an ultimate reality acting on itself is a contradiction in terms, the common ground cannot be aware of itself in an act of reflective, subject-object self-cognition. If primordial wisdom, the expression of the cognitive potency (*thugs rje'i rtsal*) [of the ground], were in itself able to actualize or realize the fundamental nature [of the ground], what would distinguish the state of the ground from that of the result?

Now when the appearances of the ground arise from the ground, two doors or possibilities present themselves: the door of freedom and the door of delusion. It is appropriate to speak in this way, for it is just as [there are two possibilities] when people encounter a mirror and see their features reflected in it. Older and more mature people recognize that it is their own appearance reflected in the mirror and are not alarmed, whereas children who do not understand this, may be frightened.

Herein lies the crucial point of the teachings [about the six special features of Samantabhadra's freedom], where it is said that the appearances of the ground are recognized as the self-experience of ultimate reality [awareness]; that this recognized appearance is superior to the ground itself; that the particular qualities of the ground are discerned; that on the basis of this discernment, freedom occurs, and so on.[101]

At that time [namely, of Samantabhadra's freedom] great primordial wisdom, the expression of cognitive potency, recognizes the entire array of the ground's appearances as its own display, the display of self-arisen primordial wisdom, the all-creating enlightened mind—in other words, the display of the dharmakāya Samantabhadra. And being endowed with decisive certainty, having thus recognized it, it lays hold of the very dharmatā itself and does not stir from it. This can be established by the ordinary mind by means of appropriate reasoning. In the moment [of recognition], all-discerning wisdom—that is, self-arising primordial wisdom (*shes rab rang byung gi ye shes*)—destroys forever all the seeds of the ignorance that has the same nature as awareness (the cause), and also of coemergent ignorance and conceptual ignorance (the conditions), with the result that the ground's appearance can never again become the ground of delusion.

In short, although the ground and result resemble each other simply by virtue of the dharmatā—that is, the inseparability of its ultimate nature, character, and cognitive potency—nevertheless, at the time of the ground, the ground [awareness] fails to recognize itself so that it is possible for it to serve as the ground of delusion. At that point, therefore, it is called the "indeterminate ground expanse" (*gzhi dbyings lung ma bstan*). And since it is the common ground of both samsara and nirvana, it is also referred to as a "such-ness that is stained." At the time of the result, the expression of cognitive potency—namely, great primordial wisdom, otherwise known as the "immaculate all-discerning wisdom"—recognizes its own nature. When this happens, the door of impure delusion is closed and the door of pure primordial wisdom dissolves into the dharmatā. It is thus that primordial wisdom takes hold of the original condition of the dharmatā. And since freedom has thus been gained in the primordially pure inner luminosity—the ever-youthful vase body[102]—this same freedom can never be lost. This is the final result, the dharmakāya endowed with the twofold purity.[103] Herein lies the difference between the ground and the result.

According to the general point of view, the manner in which the ground's appearance emerges from the ground is an immensely subtle process of dependent arising. In the last analysis, however, given that everything can arise from the dharmatā (the ultimate reality that does not exist as anything at all), the ultimate range of freedom, delusion, and of all things is found within the dharmatā. Therefore, although neither freedom nor delusion fall outside the dharmatā, which is awareness itself, if one looks at the matter from the conventional point of view, one can say that there are two kinds of buddhahood—the buddhahood of the never deluded ground, and the buddhahood of true realization.

Now with regard to the fundamental nature, the dharmatā,

As it was before, so later it will be.
It is unchanging dharmatā.

As this quotation states, there is no division possible in ultimate reality, the dharmatā. There has never been delusion in the past, there will never be delusion in the future, and in the present moment there is no delusion in the ground. The ground, therefore, is always the same. And yet, from the standpoint of the way in which phenomena appear, although previously at the time of the ground, there is no delusion in that same ground (which is primordially pure), nevertheless, with regard to spontaneous presence [the ground's appearances themselves], the seeds of delusion have not been removed. Even though primordial wisdom, as the ground for the arising of cognitive potency, is present, it has not in fact been realized, and for this reason, it is acceptable to say that the dharmatā provides the common ground for both delusion and freedom. Subsequently, however, at the time of the result, since the indwelling primordial wisdom *has* been realized, the seeds of delusion have been destroyed forever. It is like people who recover from smallpox [they can never again fall victim to the illness].

Therefore, even though ultimate reality, the dharmatā, is unconditioned, nevertheless from its state—or as its expression—all phenomenal appearances are liable to arise. This is because their fundamental nature is emptiness, freedom from conceptual construction. As it has been said,

> Where emptiness is granted,
> Everything is likewise granted.[104]

The ground expanse is not empty, however, in the sense of being a mere nothingness, for it is luminous to its core and endowed with awareness. It is for this reason that freedom, delusion, and all other states are possible. If it were no more than a mere unconditioned vacuum, the phenomenal appearances of samsara and nirvana could not arise from it. In the last analysis, it would be nothing more than the extreme of nothingness and would indeed be void of any functionality. But on the contrary—and this is the great difference—the ground is the indivisible union of the ultimate expanse and primordial wisdom; and it is thanks to this crucial fact that all phenomena—of samsara, nirvana, and the path—are able to arise from it. This ground, moreover, is the basis for the following difference of imputation [as expressed in the *Karikā*]:

> Nirvana is an uncompounded state,
> While both existent things and nonexistent things are
>   composite.[105]

If this were not the case, what would there be that might go beyond suffering, and where indeed would it go? It is with regard to the unconditioned state of union [of wisdom and the ultimate expanse] that all the phenomena of the ground, path, and result are able to arise. In relation, therefore, to both freedom and delusion, this state is causally effective. This is the meaning of the expression "The illusory vajra is the supreme ruler." Therefore, with regard to the three states of ground, path, and result, it is important to understand that appearance and emptiness are inseparably united. Just like the rainbow colors that arise unhindered when a crystal is subjected to the right conditions, all appearances (the ground's appearances and so on)—the spontaneous presence of [the ground's luminous] character—are from the very beginning and forever inseparable from the vast expanse of emptiness, the primordial purity that is the ground for their arising. If it were otherwise, the kind of mistake would occur as indicated in the text,

> Since there is no cause and no dependence on conditions,
> It must forever be or never be.[106]

Although the ground's appearances are thus present within the expanse of the ground of arising, the ground itself does not list to their side. For, by its very nature, it is emptiness and cannot be adulterated by any fragmentation or partiality.

When one considers the way in which these appearances manifest, that is to say, the various displays of luminosity, such as the ground's appearances arising within the ground—which previously were not manifest as outwardly radiating luminosity but occur at some later stage—these same appearances seem, for that reason, to be adventitious. From the standpoint of their ultimate mode of being, however, these displays are simply the spontaneous radiance of the ground, the dharmatā, the state of equality. Now since the ground nature is not something adventitious, something that [did not exist before but] is newly arisen, the displays that manifest within it cannot be separated from it as if they were of a different nature. For a detailed exposition of how the latter are self-arisen, unconditioned, and permanent, one should consult *The Cycle of the Uncontrived Mind*.[107]

It should be understood that these displays of luminosity are the effortless arising of the radiance of self-arisen primordial wisdom. They should not be regarded as conditioned phenomena endowed with specific characteristics. For if they were, all the crucial points of the definitive and secret "path of the result" would be lost. This is why it is necessary to distinguish the universal ground from the dharmakāya,[108] (ordinary) consciousness from primordial wisdom, the (ordinary) mind from awareness,[109] and so on.

In brief, in terms of their respective purity, the experiences that occur when the impure wind-mind is brought under control through the six-branch yoga [of the Kalacakra] are said to be as different from the displays of luminosity (the radiance of primordial wisdom) that manifest spontaneously and effortlessly through the profound skillful means of the Great Perfection as the earth is from the sky.

When the ground's appearances first arise within the primordial ground, the gaining of liberation or the failure to do so depends on the faculties of the person in question—which may be keen or dull in the same way that a knife may be sharp or blunt. For as it is said in scriptures such as *Summarized Wisdom* and the *All-Creating King*,[110] anything [whether freedom or bondage] can arise from ultimate reality, which does not exist as anything at all. Nevertheless, the ground itself does not, for that reason, become either good or bad. For this very ground does not fall into any extreme. For a detailed exposition of this point, one should consult *The Treasury of All Vehicles*,[111] composed by Kathok Shākya Dorje.[112]

Within the nature of unconditioned ultimate reality, there is no such thing as the duality of apprehender and apprehended. But through grasping at the appearances displayed therein as being one's own, one falls into delusion. It is like mistaking a rope for a snake. This misapprehension arises adventitiously, and yet this is nothing other than the ground's appearance, the display of the dharmatā, ultimate reality. Consequently, if it is traced back to its origin, it does not fall outside the display of the state of purity and equality of the dharmakāya.

This is why neither freedom nor delusion are posited as being within the state of the ground, the dharmatā. For within the ground there is neither freedom nor delusion. Freedom and delusion are ascribed to the appearances of the ground because it is through the recognition or nonrecognition of these appearances as the expression of the ground that freedom or delusion occur.

Therefore, although the primordial wisdom of the ground of arising is within the ground, the ground itself does not ripen into the resultant fruit because there is no all-discerning wisdom—no self-arisen primordial wisdom (*shes rab rang byung*)[113]—manifesting within it. By contrast, at the time of the result, this same all-discerning wisdom (the expression of cognitive potency), does recognize its own nature and consequently the ground ripens into the fruit. Ripening or absence of ripening has no reality from the point of view of the ultimate analysis of the dharmatā; it is spoken of only on the conventional, relative level. It is like the so-called transformation [of the mind into primordial wisdom] mentioned in the lower vehicles.

The ways in which [the appearances of] spontaneous presence arise through the eight doors[114] and so on are in general clearly explained in the tantras and the commentaries on their meaning. In particular, for a practitioner on the path, the elucidation of these ways of arising, as well as a discussion of the introduction to the nature of the mind, is to be found in *The Vision of the Net of Light*, which is part of the Heart Essence of the Ḍākinī.[115] The truth is that if what arises through the first six doors is recognized as being great primordial wisdom, the expression [of cognitive potency], and if mastery is gained of what is referred to as the "state of the natural great equality," this indeed is the door of pure primordial wisdom. If, on the other hand, it is not so recognized because of self-clinging and the dualistic cognitions of the apprehender and the apprehended, one strays into the ordinary experience of accepting and rejecting, and this is the door of impure delusion. Of course, the roots of these two doors are respectively awareness or primordial wisdom and ignorance or the deluded mind. If a proper investigation is made of how all pure phenomena (the kāyas, wisdoms, and so on) and all impure phenomena arise, remain, and subside—respectively, the manifestation of awareness and the manifestation of the ordinary mind—one will grasp the profound crucial point that is to be understood.

———————

You have asked me when it was that Garab Dorjé gained freedom—wondering whether it was at the time when Vajrasattva gave him the direct empowerment in the manner of a king, or whether it was when he finally melted into the stainless body of light.

Generally speaking, all the profound and definitive teachings of the Great Vehicle agree in saying that the supreme nirmāṇakāya, the great Shakyamuni, was manifestly enlightened from the very beginning. Therefore, the various situations of his life and deeds, appearing according to the karmic destiny of beings to be guided—from his first generation of the enlightened mind until his final awakening, the turning of the wheel of the teaching, and the withdrawal of his emanation—are all the manifestations of a single buddha. Similarly, in the context of the ultimate teachings of the uttermost secret, it is said that the teachers Samantabhadra; Vajrasattva; Vajradhara; Adhicitta, the son of the god; the nirmāṇakāya Garab Dorjé; and others are all magical illusion-like manifestations that appeared in accordance with the needs of beings. Therefore, whether they attained freedom or not in a historical sense, it is impossible to say or even imagine according to the ordinary modes of thought and speech.

From the perspective of an ordinary person, training gradually on the path, I think that with the help of the symbolic skillful means of the direct empowerment given in the manner of a king, or of an empowerment of the power of awareness, dharmatā is not left on the level of theoretical reasoning but is truly encountered and experienced. In other words, when one is introduced to the nature of the mind, one sees the dharmatā in reality. Then, in meditation, as one grows used to what one has seen, the meditative experiences of awareness (*nyams snang*) will increase with the result that awareness will be brought to its culmination. Finally, all phenomenal appearance (the expression of awareness) will dissolve into the ground, the primordial expanse where all phenomena come to exhaustion, and one will actualize the state of union of the path of no more learning in the primordial purity of inner space, the place of freedom.

What is the meaning of a direct empowerment in the manner of a king? When a *cakravartin*, or cosmic emperor, is enthroned, the divine elephant of Indra takes a golden vessel with his trunk and anoints the crown of the emperor's head, thereby empowering him to assume the lordship of his realm. In like manner, when one is directly introduced to the state of indwelling primordial wisdom and is initiated into the great primordial wisdom (the expression of cognitive potency), all that appears subsides into the state of primordial wisdom—I think that this perhaps resembles an empowerment in the manner of a king.

When one perfects the four visions of thögal, one will arise in the body of great transference. After the ground's appearances dissolve into the expanse of primordial purity, one will manifest again in a form body according to need. But since these two bodies share the same essential meaning, I think that they should perhaps be both included in the wisdom body of the state of union of no more learning.

———

"To rest in the nature of the mind once it has been seen" and "to settle completely and immediately in awareness" both come down to the same thing. For this reason, all the essential points are included in the recognition of the natural and uncontrived fundamental nature of the mind, the indwelling meditative absorption of awareness, the primordial wisdom, pure from the beginning, beyond the intellect. This is the same as saying that they are all included in the recognition of the dharmatā, the state of equality beyond the elimination of faults and the addition of qualities, and in the preservation of that state without accepting or rejecting anything. For it is said that whatever appears is but [the display of] primordial wisdom.

———

Now concerning the distinct and separate apprehension of both luminosity and emptiness, the following may be said. At first, when one receives empowerment, one relies on numerous symbolic methods for the introduction to awareness (the "fourth state," free from thoughts related to the three times). One also relies on practices such as that of the "threefold space." Thanks to these, one will have an experience of awareness that is luminous and empty— like a single ray of sunlight emerging from the clouds. But if one assumes that this is the ultimate state, and if one fails to recognize past, present, and future thoughts and all minds and mental factors as the state of the great equality of dharmatā, ultimate reality, one will cling to this luminous and empty state and will persistently separate these two aspects from each other. The eyes of one's mind will be influenced by one's wind-energy, and one will end up imagining with one's intellect precisely that which is beyond the intellect, clinging to the very state that is beyond clinging! In the end, one will fail to accomplish the Great Perfection and will achieve nothing but the disturbance of the life-wind. One will be driven insane, neither dead nor alive. This happens a great deal these days.

The truth is that one should keep to a meditation on the state of equality that is free from all partiality—a meditation that is uncontrived and that flows on like a river. If one makes many changes—suppressing this, cultivating that—this will simply be the cause of deviation; and within the blank and indeterminate state of the universal ground, which is unaware and unclear, one will fail to eliminate misconceptions about the genuine fundamental nature, with the result that the self-arisen primordial wisdom of vipaśyanā will not arise from within. One thus meditates in a state that is beyond words and formulations only in the sense that one fails to identify or recognize anything! It is based on samsara; it has the nature of ignorance! This wordless, inarticulate experience resembles the state of primordial wisdom—the state that is beyond words, thoughts, and formulation, and that arises when the power of the wisdom of vipaśyanā has been perfected and the profound, fundamental nature has been actualized just as it is—only to the extent that they are both inexpressible! They do differ, however, according to the arising or otherwise of definitive certainty with regard to the fundamental nature and in the removal or otherwise of doubts and misconceptions about it, and so on. These two states are as different from each other as are the experiences of having one's eyes open or closed. This can be understood from one's own inner experience. The latter state—that of primordial wisdom—relies on awareness, the immaculate and exalted ground of self-arisen primordial wisdom. If one grows used to this state, all-discerning wisdom (the expression of awareness), which distinguishes phenomena in terms of the specifically and the generally characterized, is able to cause all the qualities that are the signs of the path to arise effortlessly. This is why the two states just mentioned must be distinguished. Except for those who have trained in the practice of vipaśyanā in previous lives and gained experience of it, this is something that ordinary beings have difficulty in realizing, and consequently they make many mistakes. If in their meditation sessions, beginners in the practice analyze too much and worry about whether their mental state is the ordinary mind or awareness, consciousness or primal wisdom, the universal ground or the dharmakāya, they will be distracted and perturbed. These are no more than states of intellectual inquiry and are of no help in the realization of the fundamental nature of the mind. It is therefore good to bear in mind that a natural, uncontrived state of mind is the very essence of meditation. As it is said,

> If you recognize your very thoughts as dharmatā,
> No need to search for dharmadhātu somewhere else.

And as the lord Milarepa said,

> If on the inconceivable you know how you might meditate,
> The blade of your defilements rusts, its keenness gone.[116]
> But if you think, reflecting overmuch,
> However you may meditate, you're in delusion's snare.

Consequently, the inward experience of the dharmatā will gradually and inevitably lead to the certainty and conviction of it. Mere speculation on the other hand will lead nowhere.

———

Now regarding the meaning of the term *mi jé* (*mi mjed*). Action (karma) and defilement are said to be inseparable (*mi mjed*) from suffering. This word, however, also means "endurance," or "great forbearance," as has been explained in the *White Lotus*, the commentary on the *Precious Treasury of Wish-Fulfilling Jewels*[117] [by Gyalwa Longchenpa]. Personally, I have seen no other explanations of this term.

———

When one finally comes to the ultimate result, the immaculate expanse that is free of all obscuring veils, one actualizes the ultimate fundamental nature of the dharmadhātu, where appearance and emptiness are inseparably united. From the standpoint of the aspect of primordial purity, this expanse is the dharmakāya of inner luminosity. From the standpoint of the aspect of unhindered appearance—its own self-experience, spontaneously present—it is an array of the sambhogakāya buddha fields and so on. I think, therefore, that it might be best to understand that these two [kāyas: the dharmakāya and the sambhogakāya] are indistinguishable in terms of different, earlier and later, moments in time, and so on. They are inseparably united in the state of equality.

A thing seen and one who sees have no existence in the ultimate mode of being of the dharmatā. By nature they are but the same state of equality. Nevertheless, the array of enlightened bodies and buddha fields arising from the dharmatā manifest distinctly and unceasingly. Therefore, I think there is no conflict in considering the latter to be inseparable [from the dharmatā]. For the final object to be realized is pure, ultimate, primordial wisdom, which beholds the inseparability of the two truths.

Here, therefore, in answer to your questions, I have written down just what came into my mind. This is not an analytical investigation based on authoritative commentaries. And since in the conceptual mind many things are uncertain and are not susceptible to clear determination, there may well be many errors and mistakes in what I have written. Read this therefore with the pure eyes of Dharma, comparing it with commentaries that can be trusted, such as the writings of the Great Omniscient One (Longchenpa), and leave aside whatever is mistaken.

As a response to the questions of the learned Khenpo Jigme Drayang, an able exponent of the sutras and the tantras in terms of both scripture and reasoning, the dull and stupid Pema Namgyal wrote whatever came to mind while he was ill in bed. Virtue!

5

Taken from the Teachings of the Great Siddha Sherab Yarphel

Here is a short presentation of the ground, path, and result, illustrated with examples and easy to understand, taken from the writings of the greatly accomplished Sherab Yarphel, who beheld the truth of the dharmatā on the noble path.

The common *ground* [of both samsara and nirvana], the fundamental nature of the sugatagarbha, is said to be the indivisibility of primordial purity and spontaneous presence. From the standpoint of its ultimate nature, primordial purity, the sugatagarbha remains, throughout the three times, without movement or change, without increase or decrease. It is without center and circumference and is beyond all conceptual and verbal distinctions. Viewed from the standpoint of its luminous character, even though in itself it is without color or defining characteristics, it is nevertheless the ground, spontaneously present and unceasing, from which all things arise. Beyond both phenomena and the mind, the dharmatā in itself is inner luminosity, the outer seal of which remains unbroken. It is like the light of a crystal, an inwardly gathered luminosity. Whereas the dharmatā is immutable, the spontaneous display of cognitive potency manifests in various ways—the outwardly radiating luminosity unfolds as the phenomenal appearances of samsara, nirvana, and the path. If these phenomena are examined, however, they are found to be devoid of arising, remaining, and ceasing. It is just as when a ray of sunlight strikes a crystal, the latter's inner light radiates outwardly, even though, by its nature, this outward radiance is devoid of "birth."

As a way of exemplifying the *result* (the perfection of the qualities of elimination and realization), one could say that when the rays of sunlight disappear, the light of the crystal is reabsorbed into its inner luminosity.

Now, all the many stages of the *path* as they appear, from study and reflection onward, or, again, all the ground's appearances, occur within the ground—the dharmatā or awareness—which is like a white conch. And, in terms of the same example, all these stages resemble the appearance and perception of this white conch as yellow by a person suffering from jaundice. This corresponds to the universal ground and the consciousness of the universal ground, from which unfold the five sense consciousnesses and their objects, which are like the yellow color that appears to the [diseased] visual organ and that the mental consciousness takes to be truly existent.[118] Ego-clinging that arises naturally within the mental consciousness is called the "defiled mental consciousness."[119] It is like a child whose mental capacity is undeveloped and who thinks that the conch really is yellow.

In the case of ordinary people, study, reflection, and meditation on the merely intellectual level might result in just the certainty of the absence of true existence. There is no need to say that it is difficult for them to see primordial purity, the sugatagarbha. Such people are even unable to arrest deluded appearance and perception. They are like old people suffering from jaundice who, far from being able to see the color of the conch shell as it is, are unable to arrest the perception of its yellowness.

When however—through the practice of śamatha and vipaśyanā—deluded appearances and deluded apprehensions gradually diminish so that finally the view of the "single taste" is realized, the universal ground is partially cleansed and the dharmakāya or sugatagarbha becomes [partially] visible. If this is posited as the ultimate truth of dharmatā, and if the impure aspects of the universal ground are posited as relative, false, and deceptive phenomena, the matter is easy to understand. This is similar to someone being partially cured of jaundice and who, as a result, is able to discern patches of white at the edges of the conch shell, while the other areas seem yellow. Finally, when through meditating on true paths, the resultant true cessation, the dharmakāya without center and circumference, is actualized, this is like someone being entirely cured of jaundice and who can therefore see the entire conch, from its center to its edges, as completely white.

Since, as it is said, an example is able to illustrate its referent only in part—for if it were to cover every aspect of the thing it would have to be the thing itself—it is important to distinguish the two cases. And since it is in dependence on the "example wisdom" (the signifier) that the "ultimate wisdom" (the signified) is assimilated, it is said that "Thanks to the example, its referent is recognized; thanks to the reason given, conviction is gained."

On the one hand, there is the forward procedure in which the eight consciousnesses progressively unfold, together with their deluded perceptions, which constantly proliferate and become increasingly gross. On the other hand, there is the reverse procedure, thanks to which, through meditation on true paths, the eight consciousnesses diminish and become increasingly subtle until they are finally arrested. These two procedures are exemplified by the waxing and waning of the moon. By the same token, both the ground and the result can be illustrated by the inner luminosity of the black moon. So it is that if one knows how to study, reflect, and meditate, one will realize the ultimate truth.

————

There now follows a brief presentation of samsara, nirvana, and the path. From the point of view of emptiness, the ultimate nature of awareness is primordial purity and therefore it is not something that can be conceived, described, or examined. When, however, it is considered from the standpoint of appearance, although awareness, the enlightened mind, does not exist as anything whatsoever, it is, like space, the ground from which everything can arise. The creative power of awareness, the totally unobstructed power of manifestation, is like the surface of a limpid mirror completely free of stain. Its display is the array of phenomena arising as the various appearances of the universe and beings —in the manner of the eight examples of illusoriness.[120]

Now with regard to this display, both the appearance as perceived and the object of perception are posited,[121] although they exist in neither the inner nor the outer world. They occur in the manner of reflected images and are like the eight examples of illusion. Whereas in general one talks about things and their nature, in the Nyingma tradition we say instead that things are nonexistent while clearly appearing. We say, too, that main minds and mental factors occur as the impure display of the creative power of awareness.

In short, awareness exists as neither samsara nor nirvana, and yet it is the unobstructed ground from which everything arises. The creative power of awareness is that from which both samsara and nirvana can manifest. The display of this creative power is the array of clear appearances, which exist neither as the mind nor as something other than the mind, and which are empty, clear, and groundless. We should understand, therefore, that the creative power and display [of awareness] are both groundless and rootless, with the result that when freedom is gained—just as when awaking from a dream—all things and their attributes are purified into their genuine condition and there is no further stirring from the original, natural state of self-cognizing awareness, the unchanging dharmakāya.

This point may be expressed in even shorter terms. *Creative power* or *expression* refers to the ability of awareness to bring about the different manifestations of both samsara and nirvana. It is like sunlight, which causes the lotus to open and the night lily to close. *Display* refers to awareness that manifests through its radiance, just like a flame that is manifest through its glow or the sun through its rays. *Ornament* refers to the array of awareness's self-experience, which, when perceived, is an ornament for the nature of self-arisen awareness—like rainbow clouds, and the sun, moon, and stars, which adorn the sky.

———

The utterly pure ground of all objects of knowledge is referred to as the "ultimate expanse." The utterly pure minds and mental factors, which are the "knowers" or agents of knowledge, are referred to as "self-cognizing primordial wisdom."

———

At the time of the upper and lower paths [of samsara and nirvana], the nature of the mind is referred to as the "dharmatā" in reference to its empty aspect. Regarding its appearance aspect, minds and the beings endowed with minds are referred to respectively as "attributes" and the "possessors of attributes."

Moreover, from the perspective of skillful means on the relative level, one speaks of the truth of the path, or true paths, and from the perspective of the ultimate result produced by those skillful means, one speaks of the truth of cessation, or true cessations.

———

Phenomena that appear are not the mind and yet they are none other than the appearances of the mind's habitual tendencies. Consequently, if they are assessed in terms of the subject [the mind], they are qualified as empty forms. The reflected images of appearing objects (that is to say, the mind's entirely subjective experience, or perception, of such objects) are not the appearing objects themselves, and yet neither are they the appearance of something else—something different from the appearing object. Therefore, even if phenomena are assessed in terms of the object, they are also empty forms.

———

Similarly, appearances that are known to be false and without true existence are known as the "correct relative" (*yang dag pa'i kun rdzob*)." Those that are taken to be true are the "incorrect relative" (*log pa'i kun rdzob*).[122]

———

The knowledge through the mental factor of discernment (*shes rab*) that phenomena are without intrinsic being is known as the "figurative ultimate." The realization of the exalted primordial wisdom of union [of appearance and emptiness] of the same, indivisible taste of phenomena is called the "nonfigurative ultimate."

———

It is said in the tantras that "the mind is the aggregate of the four names."[123] Perception apprehends the characteristics of things and is classified as small, medium, and great. Feeling fixes on experience as being pleasant, painful, or neutral. Conditioning factors constitute manifest exertions and are the fifty-one mental factors. Consciousness is that which is aware and differentiated into eight kinds. Now, if disciples have no experience [of the view] beyond all reference, which transcends these four aggregates, the teacher will be unable to introduce them to the nature of the mind and the disciples will find it hard to understand.

In particular, when the mental consciousness dissolves into the universal ground and the latter awakens as the dharmakāya, this is called the "wisdom of emptiness." At that moment, consciousness (as one of the aggregates) ceases. As it is said in the *Ratnakuta*,[124] "Although they are free of the ordinary mind, the intellect, and the consciousnesses, they have not discarded the state of concentration. This is the inconceivable secret of the mind of the tathāgatas." Similarly, when one is free from the mental consciousness, since the latter is no longer manifest, this state is referred to as the absence of conceptual characteristics, or the absence of intrinsic being. When this happens, perception as one of the aggregates ceases. And since, at that time, there is neither inner mental experience nor some external thing apprehended, the aggregate of feeling ceases. When this happens, since all exertions related to one's expectations collapse,

and whatever arises naturally subsides, the aggregate of conditioning factors ceases. Whether these remarks are correct or otherwise
(when checked against the sutras, tantras, and pith instructions),
what I have written corresponds to my own experience.

———————

If one knows how to meditate properly on emptiness, freedom
from conceptual characteristics, and absence of expectation, one
takes hold of the path to liberation and omniscience. Without
these three doors of perfect liberation, liberation and omniscience
will be hard to gain. Why is this? It is because when one trains in
emptiness, one will accomplish the dharmakāya. If one trains in
freedom from conceptual characteristics, one will accomplish the
sambhogakāya. And if one trains in the absence of expectation,
one will accomplish the nirmāṇakāya. It may be said that the view
corresponds to emptiness, that meditation corresponds to freedom
from conceptual characteristics, and that action corresponds to
absence of expectation. Or, again, one could say that the view cannot be pointed out, that meditation is utterly beyond ["meditator
and something to be meditated on"], and that action is beyond all
expectation. All these statements are compatible with each other,
and there is no conflict between them.

As for the way of training in the three doors of perfect liberation, the following may be said. When practicing śamatha free
from distraction, one should remain in a state of natural, free flow,
without reflection and meditation, beyond hope and fear—that is,
in a state where whatever arises naturally subsides. This is a state of
natural luminosity, a wide-awake state of emptiness in which [ordi-
nary] cognition, [ordinary] thinking, and [ordinary] knowing are
no longer present.

As it is said in *Vajra Words*,[125]

> Radiance of awareness arises suddenly in the state of calm
>   abiding.
> The wide-awake awareness of it is the penetrating insight.

And,

> There is total relaxation but no clinging to it.
> There is vivid motion but no identifying it.
> There is clear subsiding but no afterthought.
> This is called spontaneous trikāya.

If, being forgetful, one is distracted from the state of calm abiding—and thinking, cognition, and knowing occur—one should understand that this is utterly undesirable.

Therefore, until one realizes that all phenomena are objects of knowledge that are devoid of arising, remaining, and ceasing, and that the mind—the knower—is also free of arising, remaining, and ceasing, the nature of the mind has not been recognized.

———

Some in their pride assert that no matter how one meditates, apart from the mental states that appear and instantaneously disintegrate, there is neither an object nor a subject of meditation. But if this state is examined, it is only the universal ground, not the dharmakāya. For when the universal ground dissolves into the dharmakāya, there still remain the appearances of luminosity to be meditated upon, even though there is no meditator—a fact that is proved by experience.

———

If, astride the horse of an unmoving śamatha, one is able, with discerning and unmistaken wisdom, to investigate effectively the four great elements (all of which are liable to destruction and disintegration) as the characteristic nature of form, the lesser elements that constitute the five sense organs and their five objects, as well as imperceptible forms and so on—if, in short, one is able to investigate both outer phenomena and the inner mind, then, aside from their different status, whether lowly or supreme, they will all be found to come down to the same point. It is as the Lord Buddha declared to Kāśyapa: "What is the wisdom that perceives all phenomena? It consists in the diligent search for the mind." He also said, "This is most difficult to realize when one's learning, reflection, and meditation do not focus on phenomena and the mind."

Whereas the ground itself is indivisible, there are, with regard to the appearances of the ground, infinite classifications, such as the successive vehicles and so on. As Maitreya has said [in the *Abhisamayālaṃkāra*],

> Because the dharmadhātu is without division,
> The buddha nature too is not to be divided.
> Yet through specific objects based on it,
> It may indeed by classified.

As one remains within the true path, concentration is achieved through śamatha, whereas power of memory is grounded in vipaśyanā. This is the teaching of the *Extensive Primordial Wisdom Sutra*.[126]

The view is the realization that the dharmatā, primordially present, empty, and luminous, is without center and circumference and is beyond all identification. Meditation is to remain without ideas, without conceptual characteristics, and without reference to anything—in a constant and undistracted mindfulness of the dharmatā. Action is to have no fixation on the view while in meditation, leaving all mental movement in a natural, relaxed, and free way. When the empty nature, the luminous character, and the all-pervading cognitive potency are blended together into a single indivisible knot, and are thus mastered, this constitutes the result.

If you become adept in this true path, which is utterly pure, it is certain that you will actualize true cessation. So keep this in your heart!

———————

These and other teachings were given by Sherab Yarphel. They are the words of one who had really beheld the truth of the dharmatā on the noble path, and for this reason, I think that they are extremely meaningful. If one studies the teachings of this lord of Dharma—such as his detailed instructions on how to preserve the naked vision of self-cognizing awareness (the highest instruction of the Great Perfection tradition), and if one studies the teachings that condense into their essential point all the instructions and directives for meditation on the pith instructions of Mahāmudrā, Mahāsandhi, and Mahāmadhyamaka, one will understand all their crucial points, and the views specific to them will be extremely clear.

6

MORE FROM SHERAB YARPHEL

The lord who, in one life, attained enlightenment,
Whose name is Prājña, meaningful to hear—
To him and to the host of all accomplished ones
I bow, requesting blessings that my mind be ripened and set free.

All you who long for liberation, this is how you should practice. To begin with, if you do not have the sublime wish to free yourself definitively from samsaric existence, then however diligent and constant you may be in your efforts to live virtuously in body, speech, and mind, all you are doing is just paying lip service, a pretense. Therefore, put your freedoms and advantages to meaningful use and, like Geshe Chengawa,[127] take joy in virtuous practice day and night.

Reflect upon the impermanence and the fragility of your life. Remember that it is not certain when your enemy, the Lord of Death, will come to you. You do not know what will come first, tomorrow or the next life. In a spirit of fear, dread, and foreboding, be like Geshe Kharak Gomchung,[128] without any interest in the appearances of the present life.

As you think about the way that good and evil actions come to ripeness, remember that all the experiences of happiness and suffering of your future lives depend particularly on your attitude and intentions. Therefore, be like Geshe Ben Gungyal[129] and refrain from mingling the slightest negative thought with any of your virtuous activities.

Mindful of the way in which the whole of samsara is defective in its nature and considering it to be therefore like a ditch of fire or a land of demons, shy away from the perfections and luxuries of this life and be instead like the young Nanda when he saw the hell realms.[130]

Since whatever hopes and expectations you may have regarding spiritual and temporal benefits will never be fulfilled according to your wishes but will only be a source of sufferings, just give up all such hopes and be like Serkyamo, who did precisely that and became much happier.

Give up the desire to protect and maintain your material possessions, hoarding your riches and increasing your profits. Be like a water bird that throws away the dead fish and lives content.

Distracted by a life companion, you will always suffer and your virtue will decline. So give up family life, and you will be as happy as if you had escaped from a snake's nest.

Live instead in solitude because it is there that meditative concentration will naturally occur, unwholesome ways will diminish, and virtue will increase. You will be like the hunter in the story who saw the advantages of solitude, lived a hermit's life, and achieved great mental stability.

On the other hand, even if you do live in solitude, if you cannot free your mind from thoughts and distractions, physically you may look like a great meditator, but your mind will be like a marketplace. On the contrary, it is your mind that should be in solitude.

In order to acquire a steady visualization, you must live alone. You should be like the girl who wore only one bracelet and achieved her every goal.

Faith is the gateway to the Dharma's light. Therefore, you should abandon sectarian attitudes toward other tenet systems and instead practice pure perception with regard to all of them.

Since the basis of all such qualities is discipline, you should treasure your vows and precepts like the apple of your eye.

Since the root of the path of the Great Vehicle is altruistic thought and deed, train your mind in precious bodhichitta, and with love and compassion, cherish others more than yourself.

The essence of the Buddha's teaching lies in its transmission and realization. Therefore, to the best of your intellectual ability, strive in studying, reflecting on, and meditating on the teachings, as well as on their explanation, practice, and associated activities.

Most important, be convinced that your root teacher is the very embodiment of all objects of refuge, and see all his works as skillful activities whereby beings may be guided. Be grateful, remembering his kindness. Transported with devotion and through the fierce power of your yearning, you will be able to transform your mind. By recalling him repeatedly without ever forgetting him, you will be able to halt your ordinary perceptions. And if, with a yearning devotion endowed with these four features, you are able to rely on him entirely and pray to him one-pointedly, you will immediately receive his blessings; your defilements will halt all at once, and your wisdom will immediately deepen. All your faults will be dispelled and your good qualities will increase like the warmth of summer. These things will arise abruptly all by themselves.

———

While you are training in meditation on the mind, do not ask yourself whether you have seen or recognized the fundamental nature. Just be without hope or fear, and stay deeply relaxed within. Do not worry about whether you are right or wrong. An important crucial point for your constant, stream-like practice is contained within these three instructions.

———

Do not try to accomplish emptiness; do not block appearances. In these two points lies the meaning, respectively, of the meditation and postmeditation periods.

In particular, do not put great effort into trying to still your mind. Do not arrest its movement, and do not cultivate mindfulness. Indeed, if your mind is still, it is vital just to leave it in its natural flow, without focusing on what appears. If your mind is in movement again it is vital to let it be, without fixating on it, without altering or manipulating it. And if you are in a mindful state, again it is vital to remain there freely without lending any strength to hope, fear, or to their antidotes. These three points are of the greatest importance. Since the results of training in *stillness, movement,* and *mindfulness* are the sambhogakāya, the nirmāṇakāya, and the dharmakāya, it does not matter in which aspect you train yourself. So do not adopt one and reject the others.

Even more important, it is inappropriate to maintain a duality of the watcher and the place or object watched. As it is said, "Do not search the watched; search the watcher."

If it is still, this mind itself, in its stillness, should do nothing but keep to its own nature. If it is moving, this mind itself, as it moves, should do nothing but keep to its own nature. If it is mindful, this mind itself, in its mindful state, should not observe anything else but keep simply to its own nature. In short, whether your mind is still, moving, or mindful, it should never have two objects of attention, such as a watcher and something watched, a meditator and an object of meditation. For if you meditate in this dualistic way, the strength to gain your freedom will be small.

Therefore, pursue your practice in the certainty that the nature, character, and cognitive potency [which differ only in the sense of being different aspects of the dharmatā] are indivisible. If you do, then stillness, movement, and mindfulness will arise as primordial wisdom.

In order to shed some light on the practice of Ayu and Mati, two lamas from Ju who are immersed in the threefold training, I, the old man Tsering Drugyal,[131] took some passages from the teachings of the great siddha Sherab Yarphel—who attained the fourth vision of the exhaustion of phenomena—and set them down in writing by the light of a butter lamp in Dechen Pema Öling, the dwelling place of that great siddha.

To meditate or not to meditate are both contrivances.
Within the natural state,
There is no meditator and no meditation.
May these grand old meditators
Find freedom from the ties of "meditation"
And seize the everlasting kingdom of the dharmakāya.

Mangalam

7

AN INSTRUCTION FOR YINOR

Namo Guru Vajradhāraya!

If you do not have a genuine determination to leave samsara forever (knowing that it is suffering by its very nature), and if you are without loving-kindness, compassion, and the precious attitude of bodhichitta (knowing that all beings are your parents), then however much you may pretend to meditate on the stages of generation and perfection, and however much you may pretend to recite prayers and mantras—no matter what you do—you cannot be on an authentic path. If you fail to keep only to what needs to be done right now (continually forgetting impermanence and death), then everything you do will be undertaken for the sake of this present life and you will never find the time to practice the genuine Dharma.

Therefore, in the beginning, do not be hasty, but get to the heart of the mind training according to the path of beings of the three scopes. This is of the utmost importance. You should thoroughly study the Mahāyāna sutras that teach this path, together with the commentaries on them composed by the learned masters of India and Tibet: general presentations and especially the *Seven-Point Mind Training*, Śāntideva's *The Way of the Bodhisattva*, Gampopa's *Ornament of Liberation*, and so on. Moreover, the instructions for the preliminary practice of the Heart Essence of the Vast Expanse[132] contain very clear explanations that are of great benefit to beginners in the practice. In order to understand it, it is very important to study it well, to take it in hand and to practice and assimilate it as much as you can.

From the taking of refuge until the practice of the tantra vehicle, you should keep as well as you can, according to your mental capacity, all the vows and precepts you have taken, minutely observing all that is allowed and all that is proscribed. If you fail in your observance of the vows, you should immediately restore them through confession and a firm decision to amend. By means of the four forces, you should recite regularly the *Confession of the Bodhisattva Downfalls* and the *Abridged and Detailed Confession Tantra* and recite the hundred-syllable mantra as much as you can.

The Lord Buddha declared that only he and others of his kind are able to be the judge of others; ordinary beings are unable to do so. Therefore, you should not look for faults and disparage either the teachings or other people but instead train impartially in faith and pure perception.

With perfect intention and practice, make sure that whatever virtue, great or small, that you accomplish (generosity and so on) becomes the path pleasing to the victorious ones. And since it is so important for the benefit of beings, even in solitude you should never overlook the attitude of a good heart and of bodhichitta; with this pure attitude, you should dedicate to others whatever virtue you may accomplish. This is crucial.

Admittedly, it is difficult to practice the generation stage in a truly perfect manner. Nevertheless, it is indispensable to have at least a simple meditation of an aspirational kind. All the important points of this path are explained in *The Fruit of the Union*[133] [*of the Generation and Perfection Stages*] by Getse Mahapandita.[134] This text elucidates all the methods for practicing the rituals according to our tradition in a way that is easy to understand. You should therefore consult it. It is also important to practice as much as you can both the vajra recitation and the vocal recitation of the mantras, which dissipate the obscurations of speech, and to master, following the instructions of the recitation manuals, all the changes in the visualization of the radiation and reabsorption [of lights according to the different activities].

Great profit is to be derived from the practice of the perfection stage endowed with characteristics; but there are great dangers also. If you fail to dispel obstacles and so on, many faults will occur and the perfection stage will be difficult to master. As for the perfection stage without characteristics—Mahāmudrā and the Great Perfection—you must lay down the proper foundations as described in authentic instruction manuals, and implement the practice from beginning to end. With regard to the Great Perfection, moreover, there exist a great many texts composed by the vidyādharas of the past. But among them all, the writings of the omniscient King of Dharma (Longchenpa), which are indistinguishable from the teachings of Samantabhadra and Vajradhara, have a particular power of blessing. They are preeminent on account of their great wealth of pith instructions, which are filled with profound key points. You should therefore look on them as the very life force of the path.

If, on the other hand, you read many other texts that are less clear, you should understand that the terminology used in other tenet systems is not the same. Moreover, on account of the differing capacities of their disciples, certain masters have given teachings with particular implied meanings. This means that by referring to the wording of such texts, you will be unable to cut through your misconceptions, and there is the danger of a rising storm of thoughts. At the present time, therefore, while you are a beginner in the practice, if you keep to a single text of authentic instructions and if you practice principally according to the instructions of your teacher, you will reap a true harvest.

Different teachers have different ways of guiding and different ways of practicing. Their main concern, however, is what we call the "mind," which is sometimes clearly aware and sometimes in dull turmoil—joyful when virtuous practice is quick to develop but unhappy when it is slow. You should examine well from where this mind arises; where it is, once it has arisen; and where it goes, when it subsides. You should look for its shape and color and whether it is always the same or different. Don't be satisfied with just theoretical knowledge; examine your own mind thoroughly. When you search for it, you do not find anything. It has no existence whatever—it does not belong to the kind of phenomena that are characterized by arising, remaining, and ceasing. The mind's nature cannot be identified, and this is said to be its "empty nature." This emptiness, however, is not just nothing—a space-like void. All the phenomena of samsara and nirvana—those that appear and those that are imputed—manifest distinctly from it, and this aspect is said to be the mind's "luminous character." No matter what thoughts, virtuous or otherwise, arise through the mind's creative power, if you watch the nature of awareness from which they arise, they will subside or fade away of their own accord. This aspect of lucid awareness is referred to as "cognitive potency," the expression of awareness. These three: the empty nature, the luminous character, and the cognitive potency are not separate from each other. They share an identical nature. They are so designated only in terms of conceptually distinguished aspects.

In short, the mind's fourth state, undistorted by thoughts of the past, present, and future—in other words, the self-arisen primordial wisdom, which is clear, lucid, limpid, and vividly awake—is the dharmakāya, indwelling primordial wisdom. This is what you have to recognize and preserve in its natural flow. Practitioners of Mahāmudrā call it the "ordinary mind," practitioners of Madhyamaka call it the "ultimate truth," practitioners of Pacification call it "the mind directly encountered," and so on. Different as these and other labels may be, the truth is that they all refer to the same thing.

When the mind is not projecting thoughts but remains calm and serene, this is "stillness." When thoughts are spontaneously projected toward the objects of the senses, this is "movement." Whether there is stillness or movement, there is a bare state of "awareness" that is aware of these two experiences. To recognize this and to settle naturally in it, watching it nakedly, is what we call "meditation," the maintaining of the practice.

At that time, no matter what thoughts expressive of the three poisons occur—desire that longs for its object, those one loves; unbearable anger toward one's enemies and so on; and the vague, oblivious state of ignorance that does not know what is to be done and what is not to be done—whatever states arise, do not alter them through the application of their antidotes; do not indulge in them or push them away. Instead, watch them nakedly, directly. They will disappear without a trace, and there will arise the clear, blissful, thought-free state of primordial wisdom. In fact, the so-called transmutation of the five poisons into the five wisdoms is but another way of saying that, by watching the nature of whichever of the five poisons occurs, it will subside. It will vanish, leaving no trace.

Whatever appearances, objects of the six consciousnesses, arise (forms, for instance, which are the objects of the eye), you should remain without hope or fear, without choosing some and rejecting others. Instead, relax in the fresh state of awareness, the seer of these states. Your fixation on them as truly existent things will be released then and there. This is what we call the "self-subsiding of the six gatherings of consciousness."

Whatever thoughts appear, be they wholesome, unwholesome, neutral, or indifferent, do not try to stop them with antidotes. Do not try to change the bad ones into good ones; do not chase after them in the ordinary way. Instead, simply relax in the nature of these thoughts, and they will subside without any antidote being used—as when a snake tied in a knot unties itself. To acquire the confidence that these thoughts in themselves can do you neither good nor harm is what is called the "confidence in the modes of subsiding of thoughts in the Great Perfection." This is a crucial point in the pith instructions of the highest, unsurpassed vehicle.

When thoughts subside, the karmic wind gathers in the central channel, and as a sign that this is happening, many visionary experiences of awareness (*snang nyams*) will occur, as well as experiences of [dualistic] consciousness (*shes nyams*), such as bliss, luminosity, no-thought, and so on. It is said that one should not cling to them as something sublime. Instead, without nourishing any conceit, one should simply meditate, causing them again and again to collapse into a naked state, empty but aware, beyond the ordinary mind. These experiences will cease, and the final realization, the actual, ultimate primordial wisdom, the truth of the path of seeing, will become manifest.

When you practice in this way, the sovereign method for dispelling obstacles and enhancing your meditation is to see your teacher as the Buddha in truth. Without ever losing such devotion, you should pray to him or her, and taking the four empowerments, you should mingle your mind inseparably with his or hers. This, you should be aware, is the life force of the path. From time to time, you should also study in detail the *Questions and Answers on Meditation*[135] by Khyentse [Jigme Lingpa].

Whatever meditative experiences occur, sublime or otherwise, do not stop them or indulge in them, but from deep inside you, let go of any hope or fear. Be diligent at all times and, as much as you are able, blend your meditation with the activities of the postmeditation period. Even if serious situations occur, don't let yourself be distracted by them, but remain firmly in the natural, uncontrived state. From time to time, you should implement whatever might strike to the essential point. For instance, you could strike at the essence through the practice of the threefold space, or come to a state of certainty by tracing everything back to awareness.

In short, by taking support of a continuous, riverlike, effortless, and perfect mindfulness, it is imperative that you train continually in bodhichitta, the precious mind of enlightenment: emptiness endowed with the core of compassion. If you do this, then—thanks to the blessings of your teacher and the strength of your meditation—understanding, experience, and realization will, after some time, arise from within. Your misconceptions will be dissipated in their own nature, and with a mind that is happy and relaxed, you will experience a profound certainty—such that you will not need to ask anyone any more questions. This I have heard from my peerless teacher, the true and perfect Buddha in person.

The teachings of the self-arisen Lotus King we now have met.
These sacred teachings we have now the power to practice.
Training in the crucial points whereby we realize openness and
    freedom,
May we, myself and others, reign in the primordial kingdom.

In order to fulfill the wish of the distinguished Yinor, I, an idle person, wrote this text on the spur of the moment and offered it to him. Virtue!

8

IN ANSWER TO A TULKU'S REQUEST

To the fundamental nature uncontrived,
Luminous and free from the beginning,
The great expanse beyond view, meditation, action,
Free of coming, free of going,
Without adopting and rejecting, I bow down.
In three words, I shall now explain
The essence of view, meditation, action.

In samsara and nirvana, all things are the mind's display.
The nature of this mind does not arise or cease,
It neither moves nor changes in the triple time.
No names, no concepts indicate it,
For it is beyond the reach of all-discerning intellect.
So rest now in the vast space of the dharmatā,
Beyond all ontological extremes.

However you may think of things,
They are not so in suchness.
However they be apprehended,
All is just delusion's snare.
In perfect suchness,
There's no realization and no absence of the same.
It's good therefore to rid yourself
Of all objectives of the ordinary mind.

This is not meditation—
All points of focus fall away.
Nor is it not meditation—
Delusion and distraction, all are pure from the beginning.
If you reach the fundamental nature
Beyond the reach of ordinary mind,
This is genuine reality.
Therefore settle in great luminosity,
Free of movement, clarity itself.

Free from the beginning,
There is nothing to be subsequently freed.
Good or bad, whatever thoughts occur—
Expressions of awareness—
All spontaneously subsides.
Abandon the contrivances of antidotes.
Change nothing, but relax
Within the nature uncontrived.

The nature of awareness, empty, luminous,
Wherein all thoughts subside as soon as they arise,
Is the primordial state of the three kāyas.
So through the direct path of the four kinds of resting
Uncontrived[136] within the natural state of mind,
Attain the great primordial secret in this very life.

In brief, all that appears is the great mudra,
The enlightened body of the deity.
Sounds and speech are empty resonance,
Enlightened speech or mantra.
All memories and thoughts, subsiding by themselves,
Are the enlightened mind, adorned with luminosity.
At all times implement the yoga of three vajras.

In order that the invitation of the supreme incarnation,
One who has the conduct of a siddha,
Should not be ignored, these casual words
Were written down by Gyurmé Pema Namgyal,
Who bears the name of "tulku."
May this virtue bring all beings to enlightenment.

Virtue!

9

An Instruction on How to Practice

Well then. The absence of all conceptual construction—that is, the mind's nature or ultimate mode of being—can be said neither to exist nor not to exist. As it is said,

> It is not existent; even buddhas have not seen it.
> It is not nonexistent; it is the ground of both samsara and
>   nirvana.

Within the primordially pure nature [of the mind], there arises the radiance, spontaneously present, of its [luminous] character, and its unobstructed expression manifests in the varied [display of phenomena]. The nature of the mind is wholly untrammeled and does not fall into the extremes either of permanent existence or of nothingness. When you meditate on it, you should not follow your past thoughts nor elicit future thoughts; neither should you be concerned with your present state of mind. The mind in its fourth state, that is, free of thoughts of these three times, unstained as it is by mental factors, is clear. Because it does not trail after the outer objects of the senses, it is lucid. Being unconfined, it is limpid. Since it is pure in being free of thoughts that lack any origin, it is vivid. And being untouched by whatever arises, it is awake.

Do not stop your thoughts; do not indulge in them. The six consciousnesses should be left free, without any specific object of meditation. Whatever wholesome or unwholesome thoughts arise, neither accept nor reject them. Just relax in their very nature. Whatever good experiences occur (such as bliss, luminosity, or no-thought), and whatever bad experiences occur (such as thoughts associated with the three poisons), do not cling to the good ones and do not shy away from the bad. Thanks to the view of great purity and the equality of phenomenal existence, the knot of duality is cut through. Desire for what is good, repugnance for what is bad, hope, fear, doubt, and anxiety—all belong to the dualistic state. If your mind slips into this, you will—as you have always done in the past—take yourself and your thoughts, the apprehender and the apprehended, as two different things. And you will wander in samsara.

Although at the level of the ultimate truth, the expanse of primordial purity, there is neither good nor evil, the relative truth never fails. Therefore, you must never belittle and neglect the law of karmic cause and fruit, but instead you should increase the accumulation of virtue until it is ocean vast. In the knowledge that all beings have been your parents, it is absolutely imperative that you have compassion and, to be more specific, the attitude of bodhichitta. If you are too tense or too loose, you will be unable to meditate properly, so maintain a balance between immoderate intensity and excessive relaxation. For in awareness, there are no targets to be aimed at; there is no tense dualistic clinging.

Begin with the cultivation of bodhichitta, and then meditate on your own incomparable teacher, the embodiment of all refuges, above the crown of your head, praying to him with a fervent devotion. Then as he melts into light and dissolves into you, let your mind mingle with his, and remain in the state of great bliss, the dharmatā beyond the ordinary mind. From time to time, visualize the circle of protection, and in particular, cultivate a sense of certainty in the view—namely, that within the state of primordially pure self-cognizing awareness, samsara and nirvana, happiness and sorrow, good and bad, gods, ghosts, demons, and all obstructing forces have no intrinsic existence whatever. This is so important. In short, abandon hope and fear, all worry and all doubt.

This was written by Padma Vija (Pema Namgyal).

10

CONCLUDING INSTRUCTION

To my teacher I bow down!

At the very outset, the door of the Dharma is the determined wish to escape from samsara. Therefore, right from the start, make sure that you assimilate the four reflections that transform your mind. The root of the path of the Great Vehicle is loving-kindness, compassion, and bodhichitta, therefore cherish others more than yourself. Bring all this to bear within your mind as much as you can. Since the swift arising of the primordial wisdom of the ultimate transmission of realization depends upon the blessing of your teacher, strike upon the essential point, which is devotion, the universal panacea, whereby you are able to look upon your teacher as the buddha, the dharmakāya itself. It is hard to bring low the mountain range of tight clinging to true existence—a habit you have nourished from beginningless time. Therefore, you must at all times turn the wheel of investigation and endeavor in the practice, regarding all phenomena of samsara and nirvana as unreal illusions.

When a firm conviction arises in you to the effect that all phenomena are empty and devoid of self, that their fundamental nature is beyond the reach of conceptual ascription and is the union of appearance and emptiness—emptiness endowed with every perfect quality—relax at ease in the natural flow of the uncontrived fundamental nature, the fourth state [of the mind], free of every thought relating to past, present, or future. The trammels of meditative concentration will be loosed then and there.

Do not get trapped in expectations and anxieties or in different kinds of alterations and changes of mind. Since all states of mental stillness and movement are never outside the dharmatā—that is, awareness, settle confidently in a state that is free of grasping and in which everything simply subsides as soon as it arises. In that state, there is no fixation on positive states of mind; they are like rainbows appearing in the sky. And since negative states of mind subside just where they are, there is no need for antidotes. Whatever arises naturally subsides, as when a knot into which a snake has been tied comes loose all by itself. And all neutral states of mind simply vanish quite naturally like clouds in the sky. All [deliberate] action and habitual tendencies naturally dissolve without leaving any trace behind, just as when one hits the surface of the water with a sword. They are naturally cleared away; they naturally subside. In the expanse of the great equality of the dharmatā, remain in a state of rest, like someone who has just finished a piece of work and is relaxed and content.

In the postmeditation periods, remember that all phenomena are like magical illusions, but do not ignore the relative truth of conditioned phenomena and strive in many ways to gather the two accumulations, clearing away the veils of obscuration.

In brief, when you are in a group of people, don't be an embarrassment to your friends. When you are alone, don't do anything to shame the enlightened ones. Practice steadily with untiring diligence for as long as you live.

Turn your mind to the Dharma, turn the Dharma to the path, and on the path, rid yourself of delusion. At all times, recite whatever prayers of aspiration you know, so that delusion arises as primordial wisdom.

Virtue!

NOTES

1. See the biography of Shechen Gyaltsap composed by Dilgo Khyentse Rinpoche in *Collected Works of Dilgo Khyentse Rinpoche* (Shechen Publications, 1994), 1:208. The full title of this text, as yet untranslated, is *mKhas shing dngos grub brnyes pa'i rdo rje'i rig pa 'dzin dbang 'gyur med padma rnam rgyal dpal bzang po slob brgyud dang bcas pa'i rnam thar nyung ngur brjod pa ngo mtshar zla ba bdud rtsi'i 'dzum phreng* (*The Blossoming Garland of Nectar of the Wondrous Moon, a brief biography of Gyurmé Pema Namgyal, the powerful holder of Vajra awareness, who was learned and attained accomplishment, together with a list of his disciples*), referred to hereafter as *The Blossoming*.

2. The numbering of the incarnations in the Shechen Gyaltsap lineage is somewhat complicated. The first in line was a master known as Aja Lama Drupwang Pema Gyaltsen (A mja' bla ma grub dbang padma rgyal mtshan). His incarnation, Pema Sangak Tendzin Chögyal (Pad ma gsang sngags bstan 'dzin chos rgyal) was referred to as Shechen Gyaltsap, the "regent of Shechen," in the sense that he was the regent or representative of the previous incarnation. The name "Gyaltsap" therefore begins only with the second incarnation and cannot, logically speaking, be applied retrospectively to the first. As the incarnation of the second Gyaltsap, Orgyen Rangjung Dorje (O rgyan rang 'byung rdo rje), Gyurmé Pema Namgyal is consequently counted as the third Shechen Gyaltsap, even though he is the fourth in the incarnation line. See Dilgo Khyentse Rinpoche, *The Blossoming*.

3. *Tshad ma rig gter*.

4. *Lam rim chen mo*.

5. A personal communication from Gelong Konchok Tendzin (Matthieu Ricard), Khyentse Rinpoche's personal attendant for many years.

6. See Dilgo Khyentse, *Brilliant Moon*, 44. A photograph of this stone is to be found on the back flap of the covers of the volumes of the Taiwan edition of Shechen Gyaltsap's complete works.

7. See Dilgo Khyentse, *Life and Times of Jamyang Khyentse Chökyi Lodrö*, 112.

8. See Dilgo Khyentse, *Brilliant Moon*, 18–70 passim.

9. The lower Vinaya lineage (*smad dul*) is the lineage of vows introduced to Tibet by the Abbot Śāntarakṣita. It is so called because after the persecution inflicted by Langdarma, this lineage survived only in the east and was revived and spread again from the lowlands of Kham. Previously, Khyentse Rinpoche had received ordination according to the upper Vinaya lineage (*stod 'dul*) associated with the Kashmiri master Śakya Śrī. See Dilgo Khyentse, *Brilliant Moon*, 52. For a more detailed explanation of the lineages of vows, see Jigme Lingpa and Kangyur Rinpoche, *Treasury of Precious Qualities*, bk. 1, 472n180.

10. Dilgo Khyentse, *Brilliant Moon*, 48.

11. Ibid., 54.

12. A personal communication from Gelong Konchok Tendzin.

13. See n. 1.

14. A master of great accomplishment and possessed of miraculous yogic powers.

15. Respectively, the sutra and tantra vehicles of the Mahāyāna.

16. The conceived object (*zhen yul*) is an idea or mental construct that is assumed to be an actual object of sense.

17. Respectively: *don lnga* (heart, lungs, kidneys, liver, and spleen) and *snod drug* (stomach, intestines, gall bladder, urinary bladder, and seminal vesicle).

18. I.e., fixed and unchanging.

19. Nonassociated conditioning factors are classified as neither mind nor form. Among the most important ones are names, acquisition, nonacquisition, syllables, and duration.

20. The view that the five aggregates of one's continuum constitute the "I" or the personal self.

21. The state of equality is synonymous with the dharmatā, the ultimate nature of phenomena.

22. The five aggregates (Skt. *skandha*, Tib. *phung po*) are form, feeling, perception, conditioning factors, and consciousness. The eighteen elements (Skt. *dhātu*, Tib. *khams*) are the six objects, the six faculties, and the six consciousnesses. The twelve sources (Skt. *āyatana*, Tib. *skye mched*) are the six faculties and their six objects.

23. This term describes all impermanent phenomena, everything produced through the coming together of causes and conditions. All such phenomena display four characteristics: birth, or arising; abiding; decay; and death, or cessation.

24. In this paragraph, the words in italics are a reference to the wording of the central statement of the *Heart Sutra*.

25. There is a danger of understanding *dualistic perception (gzung 'dzin)* too simply in terms of the interplay between the subject (the mind) and the object (an extramental thing). In fact, as Longchenpa explains very clearly, the dualism is between the subject—namely, the apprehending mind, and the object, which is not the extramental concrete entity but the cognition that arises in the first moment that an object is detected. See Longchenpa, *Finding Rest in the Nature of the Mind*, 262.

26. See *Way of the Bodhisattva*, chap. 9, v. 34.

27. Shantideva, *Way of the Bodhisattva*, chap. 9, v. 2.

28. *Chos 'byung ba med pa'i mdo.*

29. Respectively, *nam mkha' rin po che'i mdo* and *gshed dmar.*

30. This classification is known as the "three doors of perfect liberation."

31. The sutra in question is the *Lalitavistara* (*rGya cher rol pa*).

32. Dhatura (sometimes spelled *datura*) is a dangerous hallucinogenic plant said to cause delirium and horrifying visions.

33. Candrakīrti lists sixteen kinds of emptiness, which can be grouped into four kinds. See Chandrakirti and Jamgön Mipham, *Introduction to the Middle Way*, 322–23.

34. See, for example, Jigme Lingpa and Longchen Yeshe Dorje, *Treasury of Precious Qualities*, bk. 2, 257–61.

35. The reference is uncertain. Probably the author is referring to Mipham Rinpoche, but he could also be referring to Jamyang Khyentse Wangpo or Jamgön Kongtrul.

36. This is an approximate rendering of the following Dzogchen terms: *stong ha re ba, gsal sang nge ba, dvangs sang nge ba, mnyam khad de ba,* and *yangs phyal le ba.*

37. The meaning here is not completely clear. The Tibetan reads *thams cad kun yin kun min thams cad de'i ngang du rdzog pas bsgom pa la min pa med pa.*

38. One of the five great Madhyamaka arguments that establish the ultimate truth. See, for example, Shantarakshita and Jamgön Mipham, *Adornment of the Middle Way*, 151–52.

39. The main mind (*gtso sems*) is the consciousness that apprehends the simple presence of the object, while the mental factors (*sems byung*) apprehend and react to particular aspects of that object. See Jigme Lingpa and Longchen Yeshe Dorje, *Treasury of Precious Qualities*, bk. 1, 384.

40. This term indicates the mind's constructive or volitional action (Skt. *saṃskāra*, Tib. *'du byed*).

41. The three ways in which thoughts subside are as follows. First, thoughts subside through the recognition of their nature. This is like meeting an old friend. Second, they subside all by themselves, like the knots into which a snake has been tied. Finally, thoughts subside without causing any harm or good, like a thief in an empty house.

42. *sDom gsum rab dbye.*

43. I.e., between the view of Madhyamaka and the view of the Vajrayāna.

44. The path of tantra is said to be superior to that of the sutras in four ways. It is endowed with many skillful means, it is without difficulty, it is unlimited in understanding, and it is intended for beings of sharp faculties.

45. *Tshul gsum sgron me.*

46. *gDams pa 'bog pa'i rgyal po.*

47. *sNgags kyi spyi don tshangs dbyangs 'brug sgra.*

48. See Jigme Lingpa and Longchen Yeshe Dorje, *Treasury of Precious Qualities*, bk. 2, 347.

49. *kLong chen.*

50. See Jigme Lingpa and Longchen Yeshe Dorje, *Treasury of Precious Qualities*, bk. 1, 215ff.

51. See ibid., bk. 1, 217ff.

52. The four grounds of abiding (*gnas kyi sa rnam pa bzhi*) are referred to in the *Śrīmālādevīsiṃhanāda-sūtra*. Of these four, the ground of abiding of ignorance (*ma rig pa'i gnas kyi sa*) is the most powerful. It is destroyed only by the primordial wisdom of buddhahood. The wisdom of the Śrāvakas and Pratyekabuddhas is unable to destroy it, which is why their nirvana of cessation is incomplete. See Shantideva and Jamgön Mipham, *The Wisdom Chapter*, 229.

53. See Jigme Lingpa and Longchen Yeshe Dorje, *Treasury of Precious Qualities*, bk. 2, 390n192.

54. See ibid., bk. 2, 168, 263–64.

55. Respectively: *rdo rje'i sku*; *rtag pa'i sku*; *gyung drung gi sku.*

56. The fourth time, the wheel of everlasting continuity, transcends the specific and relative duration of the three times: past, present, and future.

57. See Chandrakirti and Jamgön Mipham, *Introduction to the Middle Way*, 331.

58. *Rang byung bde ba 'khor lo'i rgyud.*

59. See Jigme Lingpa and Longchen Yeshe Dorje, *Treasury of Precious Qualities*, bk. 1, 387ff., for a buddha's qualities of realization.

60. For the eight ways of arising of the appearances of the ground, see Jigme

Lingpa and Longchen Yeshe Dorje, *Treasury of Precious Qualities*, bk. 2, 238–39.

61. See ibid., bk. 2, 173–76.

62. See Jigme Lingpa and Longchen Yeshe Dorje, *Treasury of Precious Qualities*, bk. 1, 432.

63. The reference here is to one of the four noble truths, which in the present context are to be understood not as general principles but as classes of phenomena. One therefore speaks not of the truth of suffering, but rather of true sufferings, true origins, true paths, and so on, referring thereby to the constituents of the phenomenal world.

64. It is important to distinguish between the place of freedom (*grol sa*) and the ground of freedom (*grol gzhi*). The *place of freedom* is the primordial purity freed from adventitious obscuration through the completion of the path, and it is endowed with the twofold purity. In contrast, the *ground of freedom* refers to the appearances of the primordial ground. The recognition of the nature of the ground's appearances constitutes enlightenment. The failure to recognize the nature of the ground's appearances, however, results in the hallucinatory experiences of samsara, which means that the ground's appearances may also be the ground of delusion (*'khrul gzhi*). The primordial ground and the place of freedom are the same in substance, but whereas the former is indeterminate, the latter is not. See Jigme Lingpa and Longchen Yeshe Dorje, *Treasury of Precious Qualities*, bk. 2, 262.

65. The seed of coemergent ignorance refers to the possibility of failure to recognize the appearance of the ground as such.

66. Jigme Drayang was a khenpo of Gemang monastery. He became a disciple of Shechen Gyaltsap and later served as the director of the Shechen retreat center.

67. *Da lta'i sems skad cig ma*, literally, "the present moment of the mind," is a term indicating awareness as this is understood in the Dzogchen context.

68. See n. 44.

69. rGod tshang pa, 1189–1258. One of the early masters of the Drukpa Kagyu lineage.

70. Chandrakirti and Jamgön Mipham, *Introduction to the Middle Way*, chap. 6, v. 89, p. 80.

71. See Jigme Lingpa and Longchen Yeshe Dorje, *Treasury of Precious Qualities*, bk. 2, 472n634.

72. The word *kusāli* means "a beggar." It refers to those meditators who, renouncing ordinary life, live and practice in solitude.

73. See Jigme Lingpa and Longchen Yeshe Dorje, *Treasury of Precious Qualities*, bk. 1, 424–27.

74. Uttarakuru is the northern continent of the four continents that surround Mount Meru. Beings born in Uttarakuru are naturally endowed with pure discipline.

75. This appears to be an allusion to *The Way of the Bodhisattva,* chap. 9, v. 25, p. 140.

76. The master Tilopa (tenth century) and his disciple Naropa, 1016–1100, were great Indian siddhas. Naropa was the master of Marpa the Translator.

77. That is, either as a pure field, or as the world of suffering in which we live.

78. See n. 56.

79. 'Brug pa kun legs, 1455–1529. The famous "mad yogi" of Bhutan.

80. *Do ha.*

81. gLing rje ras pa, 1128–1188. A great master in the Drukpa Kagyu lineage.

82. *bsGom don drug pa.* The meaning of the title is unclear.

83. *Freedom from conceptual construction* and *one taste* are two of the four yogas of Mahāmudrā practice, the other two being *one-pointedness* and *no meditation.*

84. They have no certainty of the view.

85. In the Dzogchen context, the phrase *the plain and ordinary mind* indicates awareness, rig pa, not the ordinary mind in the usual sense.

86. See n. 83.

87. I.e., the Great Perfection.

88. I.e., fixation on what is to be adopted and what is to be avoided.

89. I.e., the intention to avoid samsara and to achieve nirvana.

90. This corresponds to the "action" of the triad view, meditation, and action.

91. Hva shang. The name of the Chinese master who visited Tibet in the eighth century and propounded a doctrine of sudden enlightenment. Rightly or wrongly, his name is associated with a meditative state of mental blankness that does not result in liberation.

92. This and the following expressions in italics refer to the four yogas mentioned earlier.

93. See n. 85.

94. 'Gyur med bstan 'phel. A great practitioner of the Great Perfection, he was also one of the thirteen great siddhas of Shechen.

95. A reference to the first Shechen Gyaltsap, Pad ma gsang sngags bstan 'dzin chos rgyal.

96. For a definition of the wisdom of the threefold space (literally, the "wisdom of the three skies or spaces"), see Longchenpa, *Finding Rest in Meditation*, 99.

97. The experience of bliss corresponds to the body and the desire realm, that of luminosity corresponds to speech and the form realm, while the experience of no-thought corresponds to the mind and the formless realm.

98. See Jigme Lingpa and Longchen Yeshe Dorje, *Treasury of Precious Qualities*, bk. 2, 155ff.

99. The four vajra principles are the four samayas of trekchö. These are discussed in detail in Longchenpa's *Precious Treasury of the Fundamental Nature* (*gNas lugs rin po che'i mdzod*).

100. For the three kinds of ignorance according to the Dzogchen teachings, see Jigme Lingpa and Longchen Yeshe Dorje, *Treasury of Precious Qualities*, bk. 2, 244.

101. For the six special features of Samantabhadra's freedom, see ibid., 240–41.

102. See ibid., 437n455.

103. The twofold purity is the naturally inherent purity (*rang bzhin rnam dag*) of the nature of the mind and the acquired purity from adventitious stains (*glo bur bral ba*).

104. Nagarjuna, *Root Stanzas on the Middle Way*, chap. 24, v. 14, p. 87.

105. Ibid., chap. 25, v. 13, p. 95.

106. This seems to be Śāntarakṣita, *Madhyamakālaṃkāra*, v. 7 (slightly altered). See Shantarakshita and Jamgön Mipham, *Adornment of the Middle Way*, 52.

107. Mipham Rinpoche, *gNyug sems skor*.

108. For the distinction of the universal ground from the dharmakaya, see Jigme Lingpa and Longchen Yeshe Dorje, *Treasury of Precious Qualities*, bk. 2, 261.

109. For the distinction of awareness from the ordinary mind, see ibid., bk. 2, 257ff.

110. Respectively, *Phyi mdo dgongs pa 'dus pa* and *Kun byed rgyal po*.

111. *Theg pa'i spyi mdzod*.

112. The identity of this master is difficult to establish. It is possible that the author of the text referred to is Horpo Shākya Dorje. He was a monk of Kathok, which is located next to the town of Horpo. He was an important scholar living in the fourteenth century and thus a contemporary of Longchenpa. Khenpo Kunzang Pelden, a disciple of Patrul Rinpoche and Mipham Rinpoche, is said to have identified himself as a later

incarnation of Shākya Dorje. See the biography of Kunzang Pelden by Samten Chhosphel in *The Treasury of Lives* (treasuryoflives.org). We are grateful to Gelong Konchok Tendzin (Matthieu Ricard) for informing us of this reference.

113. This term actually connotes all-discerning wisdom (*so sor rtog pa'i shes rab*) or self-arisen primordial wisdom (*rang byung ye shes*).

114. See n. 60.

115. *mKha' 'gro snying thig gi mthong snang 'od drva.*

116. I.e, if one meditates correctly, one's defilements will lose their power to inflict harm on oneself.

117. *Yid bzhin rin po che'i mdzod kyi rang 'grel pad ma dkar po.*

118. Altogether there are eight consciousnesses. These are the six sense consciousness (the sixth being the mental consciousness), followed by the defiled mental consciousness (*nyon yid*), followed by the consciousness of the universal ground (Skt. *alayavijñana*, Tib. *kun gzhi rnam shes*). In the present case, it is the sixth (mental) consciousness that mistakenly takes the yellow conch to be real.

119. The defiled mental consciousness (*nyon yid*) is the mental consciousness that constantly conceives of "I," the ego.

120. The eight examples of illusion (dream, magical illusion, trick of sight, mirage, reflected moon, echo, city of gandharvas, emanated apparition) are discussed at length in Longchenpa, *Finding Rest in Illusion.*

121. For the difference between the object of perception (*snang yul*) and the appearance as perceived (*snang ba*), see Jigme Lingpa and Longchen Yeshe Dorje, *Treasury of Precious Qualities*, bk. 2, 248–49.

122. This interpretation of the correct and incorrect relative seems to be the reverse of the usual definition.

123. I.e., the four name aggregates are feeling, perception, conditioning factors, and consciousness.

124. *dKon mchog brtsegs pa.*

125. *rDo rje'i tshig.*

126. *Ye shes rgyas pa.*

127. Chengawa Tshultrim Bar (1033–1103). He was the youngest of the "three Kadam brothers" (the others being Potowa Rinchen Sal and Phuchungwa Shönu Gyaltsen), the three principal disciples of Dromtönpa Gyalwa'i Jungé (1006–1064). See Atiśa and Dromtönpa, *Book of Kadam*, 456n469, 581, 659n533; Patrul Rinpoche, *Words of My Perfect Teacher*, 37, 210, 241.

128. Kharak Gomchung Wangchuk Lodrö (eleventh century) also known as Kharakpa, who was a disciple of Gönpawa (1016–1082), who was a disciple of both Atiśa (982–1055) and Dromtönpa. See Atiśa and Dromtönpa, *Book of Kadam*, 590–91, 601–8, 661n547; Patrul Rinpoche, *Words of My Perfect Teacher*, 59, 256.

129. Ben Gungyal Tsultrim Gyalwa, a disciple of Gönpawa. See Atiśa and Dromtönpa, *Book of Kadam*, 660n546; Patrul Rinpoche, *Words of My Perfect Teacher*, 127.

130. See Patrul Rinpoche, *Words of My Perfect Teacher*, 95–96.

131. This was the birth name of Shechen Gyaltsap.

132. I.e., *kLong chen snying thig*. The text referred to here, namely, instructions on the preliminary practice of this cycle, was composed by Patrul Rinpoche and entitled *Kun bzang bla ma'i zhal lung*, *The Words of My Perfect Teacher*.

133. *Zung 'jug snye ma.*

134. dGe rtse pan chen 'gyur med tshe dbang mchog grub, 1761–1829. A scholar and master of Kathok monastery in eastern Tibet. He was famous for arranging the carving of the blocks for the *Collection of Nyingma Tantras* (*rNying ma rgyud 'bum*) and printing the works of Longchenpa and Jigme Lingpa.

135. *sGom phyogs dri len.*

136. *cog bzhag bzhi.*

BIBLIOGRAPHY

SOURCES IN TIBETAN

Dilgo Khyentse Rinpoche. *mKhas shing dngos grub brnyes pa'i rdo rje'i rig pa 'dzin dbang 'gyur med padma rnam rgyal dpal bzang po slob brgyud dang bcas pa'i rnam thar nyung ngur brjod pa ngo mtshar zla ba bdud rtsi'i 'dzum phreng*. Shechen Publications, 1994.

Shechen Gyaltsap, Gyurmé Pema Namgyal. *Sems don dngos gzhi'i nyams len gnad bsdus rab gsal sgron me*. In *Zhe chen rgyal tshab kyi bka''bum*, vol. 1. Paro: Ngodup, 1975–1994.

———. *Sems don dngos gzhi'i nyams len gnad bsdus rab gsal sgron me*. In *Zhe chen rgyal tshab 'gyur med pad ma rnam rgyal dpal bzang po mchog gi gsung 'bum rin po che*, vol. 9. Taiwan: Corporate Body of the Buddha Educational Foundation, 2014.

Sonam Chöpel. *dPal dgon bla ma 'gyur med padma rnam rgyal gyi rnam thar mdor bsdus 'jam mgon rnam gnyis kyi zhal lung ma bcos zla ba'i rang mdangs*. Taiwan: Corporate Body of the Buddha Educational Foundation, 2014.

SOURCES IN ENGLISH TRANSLATION

Atiśa and Dromtönpa. *The Book of Kadam: The Core Texts*. Translated by Thupten Jinpa. Boston: Wisdom Publications, 2008.

Chandrakirti and Jamgön Mipham. *Introduction to the Middle Way*. Translated by the Padmakara Translation Group. Boston: Shambhala Publications, 2004.

Dilgo Khyentse. *Brilliant Moon: The Autobiography of Dilgo Khyentse*. Translated and compiled by Ani Jinba Palmo. Boston: Shambhala Publications, 2008.

———. *The Life and Times of Jamyang Khyentse Chökyi Lodrö: The Great Biography by Dilgo Khyentse Rinpoche and other stories*. Translated by

Drubgyud Tenzin Rinpoche and Khenpo Sonam Phuntsok. Boulder, CO: Shambhala Publications, 2017.

Jigme Lingpa and Longchen Yeshe Dorje, Kangyur Rinpoche. *Treasury of Precious Qualities*. 2 vols. Translated by the Padmakara Translation Group. Boston: Shambhala Publications, 2010–2013.

Longchenpa. *Finding Rest in Illusion*. Translated by the Padmakara Translation Group. Boulder, CO: Shambhala Publications, 2018.

———. *Finding Rest in Meditation*. Translated by the Padmakara Translation Group. Boulder, CO: Shambhala Publications, 2018.

———. *Finding Rest in the Nature of the Mind*. Translated by the Padmakara Translation Group. Boulder, CO: Shambhala Publications, 2017.

Nagarjuna. *The Root Stanzas of the Middle Way: The Mulamadhyamaka-karika*. Translated by the Padmakara Translation Group. Boulder, CO: Shambhala Publications, 2016.

Patrul Rinpoche, Orgyen Jigmé Chökyi Wangpo. *The Words of My Perfect Teacher*. Translated by the Padmakara Translation Group. Boston: Shambhala Publications, 1998.

Shantarakshita and Jamgön Mipham. *The Adornment of the Middle Way*. Translated by Padmakara Translation Group. Boston: Shambhala Publications, 2010.

Shantideva. *The Way of the Bodhisattva*. Translated by the Padmakara Translation Group. Boulder, CO: Shambhala Publications, 2006.

Shantideva and Jamgön Mipham. *The Wisdom Chapter*. Translated by the Padmakara Translation Group. Boulder, CO: Shambhala Publications, 2017.

THE PADMAKARA TRANSLATION GROUP TRANSLATIONS INTO ENGLISH

The Adornment of the Middle Way. Shantarakshita and Mipham Rinpoche. Boston: Shambhala Publications, 2010.

Counsels from My Heart. Dudjom Rinpoche. Boston: Shambhala Publications, 2003.

Enlightened Courage. Dilgo Khyentse Rinpoche. Ithaca, NY: Snow Lion Publications, 2006.

The Excellent Path of Enlightenment. Dilgo Khyentse. Ithaca, NY: Snow Lion Publications, 1996.

A Feast of the Nectar of the Supreme Vehicle. Maitreya and Jamgön Mipham. Boulder, CO: Shambhala Publications, 2018.

Finding Rest in Illusion. Longchenpa. Boulder, CO: Shambhala Publications, 2018.

Finding Rest in Meditation. Longchenpa. Boulder, CO: Shambhala Publications, 2018.

Finding Rest in the Nature of the Mind. Longchenpa. Boulder, CO: Shambhala Publications, 2017.

A Flash of Lightning in the Dark of Night. The Dalai Lama. Boston: Shambhala Publications, 1993. Republished as *For the Benefit of All Beings.* Boston: Shambhala Publications, 2009.

Food of Bodhisattvas. Shabkar Tsogdruk Rangdrol. Boston: Shambhala Publications, 2004.

A Garland of Views: A Guide to View, Meditation, and Result in the Nine Vehicles. Padmasambhava and Mipham Rinpoche. Boston: Shambhala Publications, 2015.

A Guide to the Words of My Perfect Teacher. Khenpo Ngawang Pelzang. Translated with Dipamkara. Boston: Shambhala Publications, 2004.

The Heart of Compassion. Dilgo Khyentse. Boston: Shambhala Publications, 2007.

The Heart Treasure of the Enlightened Ones. Dilgo Khyentse and Patrul Rinpoche. Boston: Shambhala Publications, 1992.

The Hundred Verses of Advice. Dilgo Khyentse and Padampa Sangye. Boston: Shambhala Publications, 2005.

Introduction to the Middle Way. Chandrakirti and Mipham Rinpoche. Boston: Shambhala Publications, 2004.

Journey to Enlightenment. Matthieu Ricard. New York: Aperture Foundation, 1996.

Lady of the Lotus-Born. Gyalwa Changchub and Namkhai Nyingpo. Boston: Shambhala Publications, 2002.

The Life of Shabkar: The Autobiography of a Tibetan Yogin. Ithaca, NY: Snow Lion Publications, 2001.

Nagarjuna's Letter to a Friend. Longchen Yeshe Dorje, Kangyur Rinpoche. Ithaca, NY: Snow Lion Publications, 2005.

The Nectar of Manjushri's Speech. Kunzang Pelden. Boston: Shambhala Publications, 2010.

The Root Stanzas of the Middle Way. Nagarjuna. Boulder, CO: Shambhala Publications, 2016.

A Torch Lighting the Way to Freedom. Dudjom Rinpoche, Jigdrel Yeshe Dorje. Boston: Shambhala Publications, 2011.

Treasury of Precious Qualities. 2 vols. Boston: Shambhala Publications, 2010–2013.

The Way of the Bodhisattva. Shantideva. Rev. ed. Boulder, CO: Shambhala Publications, 2008.

White Lotus. Jamgön Mipham. Boston: Shambhala Publications, 2007.

Wisdom: Two Buddhist Commentaries. Khenchen Kunzang Pelden and Minyak Kunzang Sonam. Dordogne: Éditions Padmakara, 1999.

The Wisdom Chapter: Jamgön Mipham's Commentary on the Ninth Chapter of "The Way of the Bodhisattva." Jamgön Mipham. Boulder, CO: Shambhala Publications, 2017.

The Wish-Fulfilling Jewel. Dilgo Khyentse. Boston: Shambhala Publications, 1988.

The Words of My Perfect Teacher. Patrul Rinpoche. New Haven, CT: Yale University Press, 2010.

Zurchungpa's Testament. Zurchungpa and Dilgo Khyentse. Ithaca, NY: Snow Lion Publications, 2006.

Index